Knit Now!

Knit Now!

26 Projects for Baby, Home, Gifts and More

by Candi Jensen

KRAUSE PUBLICATIONS
CINCINNATI, OHIO

www.fwmedia.com

14 13 12 11 10   5 4 3 2 1

DISTRIBUTED IN CANADA BY FRASER DIRECT
100 Armstrong Avenue
Georgetown, ON, Canada L7G 5S4
Tel: (905) 877-4411

DISTRIBUTED IN THE U.K. AND EUROPE BY DAVID & CHARLES
Brunel House, Newton Abbot, Devon, TQ12 4PU, England
Tel: (+44) 1626 323200, Fax: (+44) 1626 323319
Email: postmaster@davidandcharles.co.uk

DISTRIBUTED IN AUSTRALIA BY CAPRICORN LINK
P.O. Box 704, S. Windsor NSW, 2756 Australia
Tel: (02) 4577-3555

Library of Congress Cataloging in Publication Data
Jensen, Candi.
  Knit now : 26 projects for baby, home, gifts and more / Candi Jensen.
-- 1st ed.
     p. cm.
  "26 projects for baby, home, gifts and more."
  Includes bibliographical references and index.
  ISBN-13: 978-1-4402-1387-8 (pbk. : alk. paper)
  ISBN-10: 1-4402-1387-9 (pbk. : alk. paper)
  1. Knitting--Patterns. I. Knit and crochet now (Television program) II.
Title. III. Title: Knit now.
  TT825.J4822 2010
  746.43'041--dc22   2010004295

Edited by Liz Casler
Designed by Dawn DeVries Sokol
Production coordinated by Greg Nock
Photography by Kathleen Lussier-West and Jack Deutsch Studio

Metric Conversion Chart

To convert	to	multiply by
Inches	Centimeters	2.54
Centimeters	Inches	0.4
Feet	Centimeters	30.5
Centimeters	Feet	0.03
Yards	Meters	0.9
Meters	Yards	1.1

About the Author

Candi Jensen is Executive Producer of the Public Television series *Knit and Crochet Now*. She has had more than 300 designs published in magazines including *Good Housekeeping*, *Better Homes & Gardens* and *Family Circle* and is the author of thirteen books. With appearances on television programs such as *Knitty Gritty* and *The Carol Duvall Show*, Candi has inspired viewers with innovative ways to use knit and crochet. She works tirelessly to promote both knitting and crochet through and for charitable organizations.

Candi was born and raised in Southern California and currently resides in Northern California with her husband Tom, 1 cat and her 5 grandchildren close by.

For more information on *Knit and Crochet Now* visit www.knitandcrochetnow.com.

Acknowledgments

They say it takes a village to raise a child and I think the same holds true for this book. To begin with I want to thank the talented Brett Bara, host of *Knit and Crochet Now*. Her talent and creativity can be seen in every episode of the show. I'd also like to thank the brilliant experts on the show, Kristin Nicholas, Maggie Pace, Robyn Chachula, Drew Emborsky and our newest addition, Myra Wood. Not only have they contributed designs to this book, but they impart their wisdom to us on every show.

I am also grateful to the many other designers whose work is featured on the show and in the pages of this book. They are talented and I am so very lucky to work with them.

There are many other people who have had a hand in bringing this book to fruition and I want to thank every one at F+W Media for making this project a reality—especially Liz Casler who was able to make sense of the chaos that I handed her. A big thank you to Christine Doyle who managed to work at lightning speed to move this project forward and also to Sara Domville who saw the value of bringing the TV show into print.

As with all my other books my husband Tom has been my biggest cheerleader and makes a wonderful warm vegetable salad when I'm too tired or busy to participate in dinner. I also want to thank my new partner, Susan Levin, who has brought so much to the show in such a short time. A big hug to my daughter, son-in-law and grandchildren who are the sparkle in my life and to my friends who put up with my absence on so many occasions.

Last but not least I want to thank Rick Caron who gave me the push to produce the television show because he knew I could do it.

Dedication

This book is dedicated to all the knitters and crocheters who love their craft, are always seeking new inspiration and are eager to learn more. You are the reason *Knit and Crochet Now!* is such a success and why we love to come into your homes to bring you new designs and techniques.

Contents

Introduction

When we first came up with the idea of a television show that would feature knitting and crochet we knew it had to not only have great techniques but also truly wonderful patterns that utilized those techniques. Those two things together form the foundation for *Knit and Crochet Now* (formerly *Knit and Crochet Today*), and we keep them in mind every time we sit down to work on what we will feature in the next season of the show. The name of the show may have changed with our third year but not our dedication to bringing you the best in techniques and patterns.

This book is a compilation of knit projects from the first three seasons of *Knit and Crochet Now*—a sort of best-of-the-show. You will also find a few extra patterns that didn't appear on the show but are just too good not to share with you. We've included projects for babies and the home, accessories and gifts as well as wearables. Projects range in difficulty from easy to intermediate. As you work your way through this book we hope you will enjoy the projects and share them with the people you love. And don't forget to look for us on your local public television station!

Whether you're a longtime viewer or new to the show, you may want to check out the episode on which each of these patterns was featured. Use the episode list below as a handy guide for the projects and their corresponding shows.

Episode Guide

Chapter One

Baby Time

I have always loved designing for babies and feel a great sense of joy when I see babies and toddlers in something handmade. It's so satisfying to think about the care and time that goes into a beautiful sweater or a pair of fun booties, or that blanket that you know will be dragged around and loved over the years. The designs in this chapter are no exception and the designers have taken care to make wearable, usable and durable projects that will stand the test of time. So pick up your needles and get ready to stitch up a bunny, a bib or a blankie!

Sleepy Bunny

Soft and cuddly and ready to be loved, our rabbit friend is the perfect huggable size for your favorite baby. Our playtime pal will stitch up quickly with just a few simple shaping techniques.

Design by **Susan B. Anderson for Spud & Chloë**
Finished Measurements:
3" wide × 7" tall (8cm × 18cm)
Difficulty: **Intermediate**

Materials List

YARN

1 skein Spud & Chloë Sweater (55% super-wash wool, 45% organic cotton, 160yd [144m]) in color 7500 Ice Cream

NEEDLES & NOTIONS

1 set of 4 size US 5 (13.75mm) double-pointed needles (dpns)

Yarn needle

Scissors

Tape measure or ruler

Small amount polyester fiberfill

Tennis ball (optional)

Black embroidery floss

Stitch marker

Stitch holder or waste yarn

GAUGE

6 sts = 1" (3cm) in Stockinette stitch

Body

Starting at the bottom of the body, cast on 9 sts placing 3 sts on each of three dpns. Join to work in the round being careful not to twist the sts. Place a stitch marker on the first stitch.

Rnd 1: Knit.
Rnd 2: (K1, M1, k1, M1, k1) repeat to the end of the round (5 sts per needle, 15 sts total).
Rnd 3: Knit.
Rnd 4: (K1, M1, knit to the last stitch on the needle, M1, k1) repeat on each needle.
Rnd 5: Knit.
Repeat rounds 4 and 5 until there are 15 sts on each needle, 45 sts total. End with a Round 4. Place a stitch marker on the last completed round and leave it there.

Knit every round until the body measures 1½" (4cm) above the stitch marker.

Decrease rounds

Rnd 1: (K3, k2tog) repeat to the end of the round—36 sts.
Rnd 2: (K2, k2tog) repeat to the end of the round—27 sts.

At this point, place the end from the cast-on stitches on a yarn needle. Gather up and close the hole at the cast-on end of the Body. Pull the end to the inside and trim.

Sleepy Bunny

Insert the tennis ball into the Body and continue knitting around the tennis ball to the end. This is a little awkward but there are only a few rounds left. The other option is to stuff the Body with fiberfill at this time and continue stuffing until the last round. Stuff the Body until it is firm.

Rnds 3 and 4: Knit.

Rnd 5: (K1, k2tog) repeat to the end of the round—18 sts.

Rnd 6: Knit.

Rnd 7: (K2tog) repeat to the end of the round—9 sts.
Cut the yarn and place the end on a yarn needle. Pull through the remaining stitches and pull up tight to close the hole. Pull the end to the inside and trim.

Arm (make 2)

Next up are the Arms and Bottom Paws. You can wait until after the Head is attached to place the Arms and Paws or you can attach them as they are completed.

Cast on 4 sts on each of three dpns, 12 stitches total. Join to work in the round being careful not to twist the stitches. Place a stitch marker on the first stitch.

Rnds 1–10: Knit.

Rnd 11: (K2, k2tog) on each needle—9 sts.
Cut the yarn and pull through the remaining stitches. Pull up tight to close the hole and take a few stitches to secure. Pull the end to the inside, weave in the end and trim. Stuff the Arm lightly with fiberfill and whipstitch the cast-on end closed. Whipstitch the Arm to the Body using the photo as a guide. I attached the Arms at a slight angle so the Arms would hang forward.

Bottom Paw (make 2)

Cast on 5 stitches on each of three dpns, 15 stitches total. Join to work in the round being careful not to twist the stitches. Place a stitch marker on the first stitch.

Rnds 1–7: Knit.

Rnd 8: (K3, k2tog) on each needle—12 sts.

Rnd 9: (K2, k2tog) on each needle—9 sts.
Cut the yarn and pull through the remaining stitches. Pull up tight to close the hole and take a few stitches to secure. Pull the end to the inside, weave in the end and trim. Stuff the Paw lightly with fiberfill and whipstitch the cast-on end closed. Whipstitch the Paw to the bottom front of the Body using the photo as a guide. I attached the Paws at a slight angle so they would point slightly out.

Head:

Starting at the bottom of the Head, cast on 9 sts placing 3 sts on each of three needles. Join to work in the round being careful not to twist the stitches. Place a stitch marker on the first stitch.

Rnd 1: Knit.

Rnd 2: Kfb in each stitch—6 sts per needle, 18 sts total.

Rnd 3: Knit.

Rnd 4: Kfb in each stitch—12 sts per needle, 36 sts total.
Place a stitch marker on Round 4 and leave it there. Knit every round until the head measures 1 1/2" (4cm) above the stitch marker.

Decrease

Rnd 1: (K4, k2tog) repeat to the end of the round—30 sts.

Rnd 2: (K3, k2tog) repeat to the end of the round—24 sts.
At this time place the end from the cast-on stitches onto a yarn needle. Take several stitches to gather and close the hole at the base of the Head. Pull the end to the inside and trim. Stuff the Head with fiberfill until firm.

Ears (Make 2)

Continuing on, place the first 12 stitches on three dpns, placing 4 sts on each needle. Leave the other 12 sts on a stitch holder or waste yarn.

Join to work in the round the 12 stitches on the needles. Knit 6 rounds.

Next Rnd: (K1, M1, k2, M1, k1) on each needle (6 sts per needle, 18 sts total).

Knit every round until the ear measures 2 $\frac{1}{4}$" (6cm) from the beginning of the ear.

Decrease for the top of the ear as follows:

Rnd 1: (K4, k2tog) on each needle—15 sts.

Rnd 2: (K3, k2tog) on each needle—12 sts.

Rnd 3: (K2, k2tog) on each needle—9 sts.

Cut the yarn and place the end on a yarn needle. Pull through the remaining stitches and pull up tight to close the hole. Stitch to secure and pull the end to the inside. I pulled the end back through the bottom front of the Ear and took several stitches to pull the bottom of the Ear edges together. Pull the end to the inside and trim. Reattach the yarn in between the Ears leaving a 6" (15cm) end on the outside of the Head (this end will be used later). Place the 12 stitches from the stitch holder or waste yarn onto three dpns (4 sts per needle).

Finishing

Finish stuffing the Head. Do not stuff the bunny ears. Place the end from the reattached yarn on a yarn needle and take a few stitches to close the gap in between the Ears. Pull the end to the inside and trim to stay inside. Place a length of yarn on a yarn needle and whipstitch the Head to the top of the Body. Pull the end to the inside and trim.

Running Stitch

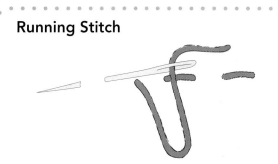

Carry the needle in and out of the material making small up and down even stitches. Take several stitches with the needle before drawing the thread through.

Tail

Make a 1" (3cm) pom-pom with 50 wraps. Attach at the lower back of the Body. Attach the Tail last and place it to assure that Sleepy Bunny can stand up on its own.

Face

Use the black embroidery floss and the yarn needle to stitch the Face. Take running stitches (see above) to make the Eyes and Nose. Pull the ends to the inside and trim. Use the photo as a guide.

Baby Afghan Square of the Week

Bundle up the baby in this charming sampler blanket and learn new stitches while you're at it. The squares have basic to intermediate techniques so you can start off slow and learn something new on each square. This is a perfect baby shower gift. Every guest can work on a different square according to her abilities.

Finished Measurements: **30" × 40" (76cm × 102cm) including border**
Difficulty: **Squares range from Beginner to Intermediate**

Materials List

YARN
Red Heart Soft (100% acrylic, 256yd [230m])
- 2 balls in color 2541 Blue Sky (A)
- 1 ball in color 9820 Mid Blue (B)
- 1 ball in color 4600 White (C)

NEEDLES & NOTIONS
Size US 8 (5mm) knitting needles
Cable needle
Yarn needle

GAUGE
16½ sts = 4" (10cm) in pattern
Each square measures about 10" × 10" (26 × 26cm)

Notes
This afghan is made from 12 squares—2 squares each of 6 different stitch patterns.

 See the included DVD to watch the episode segments for these afghan squares.

When working on a square with two colors of yarn, carry the color you are not using up the side. Then when you sew the squares together the yarn that you have carried becomes part of the seam.

Eyelet Hearts (make 2)
Make one square with C and one square with A. Multiple of 12 sts + 3.

Pattern Stitches
SKP (slip, knit, pass slipped st over) Slip 1 st as if to knit, k1, pass slipped st over knit st and off needle—1 st decreased.
SK2P (slip, knit 2 together, pass slipped st over) Slip 1 st as if to knit, k2tog, pass slipped st over knit st and off needle—2 sts decreased.

Cast on 39 sts.
Row 1: and all Wrong Side rows (WS): Purl.
Row 2: K2, *yo, k2tog, k3, yo, k1, yo, k3, SKP, yo, k1; rep from * to last st, k1—41 sts.
Row 4: K2, *k1, yo, k4tog, yo, k3, yo, k4tog-tbl, yo, k2; rep from * to last st, k1—39 sts.
Row 6: K2, *k1, k2tog, yo, k5, yo, SKP, k2; rep from * to last st, k1.
Row 8: K2, *k2tog, yo, k7, yo, SKP, k1; rep from * to last st, k1.
Row 10: K1, k2tog, yo, k9, yo, *sk2p, yo, k9, yo; rep from * to last 3 sts, SKP, k1.

Row 11: Purl.
Rep Rows 2–11 until piece measures 10" (26cm) from beginning. End with a Row 5.
Bind off.

Rosebud Trellis (make 2)
Multiple of 6 sts + 1.

Special Stitches
MB (make bobble) *K1 but do not sl st from needle, sl new st from right-hand needle to left-hand needle; rep from * four more times (working into new st each time)—4 sts increased. K6, then pass the 2nd, 3rd, 4th, 5th, and 6th st on right-hand needle over first st and off needle.

With A, cast on 43 sts.
Row 1 (WS): With A, purl.
Row 2: With A, k1, sl2wyif, yb, *MB, sl5wyif, yb; rep from * to last 4 sts, MB, sl2wyif, yb, k1.
Row 3: With A, p1, sl2wyib, *p1, sl5wyib; rep from * to last 4 sts, p1, sl2wyib, p1.
Row 4: With B, knit.
Row 5: With B, purl.
Rows 6 and 7: Rep Rows 4 and 5.
Row 8: With B, k5, *insert right-hand needle from front under top loose A strand and k next st, hooking strand behind st as it's knit; in same way, insert right-hand needle under both A strands and k next st, then under top A strand again and k next st, k3; rep from * to last 2 sts, k2.
Row 9: With B, purl.
Row 10: With A, k1, *sl5wyif, MB; rep from * to last 6 sts, sl5wyif, k1.
Row 11: With A, p1, *sl5wyib, p1; rep from * to last 6 sts, sl5wyib, p1.
Rows 12–15: With B, rep Rows 4–7.

Row 16: With B, k2, insert right-hand needle from front under top loose A strand and k next st, hooking strand behind st as it's knit; in same way, insert right-hand needle under both A strands and k next st, then under top A strand again and k next st, *k3, insert right-hand needle from front under top loose A strand and k next st, hooking strand behind st as it's knit; in same way, insert right-hand needle under both A strands and k next st, then under top A strand again and k next st; rep from * to last 2 sts, k2.
Row 17: With A, purl.
Rep Rows 2–17 until piece measures 10" (26cm) from beginning. End with a Row 9 or 17.
Bind off.

Big Bamboo (make 2)
Make one square with C and one square with A.
Multiple of 12 sts + 4

Cast on 40 sts.
Row 1 (RS): K2, *p2, k4; rep from * to last 2 sts, k2.
Row 2: K2, *p4, k2; rep from * to last 2 sts, k2.
Rows 3 and 4: Rep Rows 1 and 2.
Row 5: K2, *p8, k4; rep from * to last 2 sts, k2.
Row 6: K2, *p4, k8; rep from * to last 2 sts, k2.
Rows 7–10: Rep Rows 1–4.
Row 11: K2, p2, k4, *p8, k4; rep from * to last 8 sts, p6, k2.
Row 12: K8, p4, *k8, p4; rep from * to last 4 sts, k4.
Rep Rows 1–12 until piece measures 10" (26cm) from beginning.
Bind off.

Horseshoe Cable (make 2)
Make one square with C and one square with A.
Multiple of 18 sts + 6.

Special Stitches

6-st RC (3 over 3 right cross) Slip 3 sts to cable needle and hold in back, k3, then k3 from cable needle.

6-st LC (3 over 3 left cross) Slip 3 sts to cable needle and hold in front, k3, then k3 from cable needle.

Cast on 42 sts.

Row 1 (RS): Knit.

Row 2: Purl.

Row 3: K6, *6-st RC, 6-st LC, k6; rep from * across.

Rows 4–7: Rep Rows 1 and 2 twice.

Row 8: Purl.

Rep Rows 1–8 until piece measures 10" (26cm) from beginning, end with a Row 6.

Bind off.

Peas and Carrots (make 2)

Multiple of 4 sts + 2.

Cast on 42 sts.

Row 1 (WS): With A, purl.

Row 2: With B, k1, sl1wyib, *k2, sl2wyib; rep from * to last 4 sts, k2, sl1wyib, k1.

Row 3: With B, p1, sl1wyif, p2, *sl2wyif, p2; rep from * to last 2 sts, sl1wyif, p1.

Row 4: With A, knit.

Row 5: With C, *p2, sl2wyif; rep from * to last 2 sts, p2.

Row 6: With C, k2, *sl2wyib, k2; rep from * across.

Rep Rows 1–6 until piece measures 10" (26cm) from beginning.

Bind off.

Bean Sprouts (make 2)

Multiple of 6 sts + 5.

With A, cast on 41 sts.

Row 1 (RS): With A, knit.

Row 2: With A, purl.

Row 3: With B, k2, *sl1wyib, k1; rep from * to last 3 sts, sl1wyib, k2.

Row 4: With B, k2, sl1wyif, *k1, sl1wyif, p1, sl1wyif, k1, sl1wyif; rep from * to last 2 sts, k2.

Row 5: With A, k2, *k3, sl1wyib, k2; rep from * to last 3 sts, k3.

Row 6: With A, p3, *p2, sl1wyif, p3; rep from * to last 2 sts, p2.

Rows 7 and 8: Rep Rows 5 and 6.

Rows 9 and 10: Rep Rows 1 and 2.

Row 11: With C, *k1, sl1wyib; rep from * to last st, k1.

Row 12: With C, k1, sl1wyif, p1, *[sl1wyif, k1] twice, sl1wyif, p1; rep from * to last 2 sts, sl1wyif, k1.

Row 13: With A, k2, *sl1wyib, k5; rep from * to last 3 sts, sl1wyib, k2.

Row 14: With A, p2, sl1wyif, *p5, sl1wyif; rep from * to last 2 sts, p2.

Rows 15 and 16: Rep Rows 13 and 14.

Rep Rows 1–16 until piece measures 10" (26cm) from beginning, end with a Row 8 or a Row 16.

Bind off.

Finishing

Arrange squares in four rows of three squares each. With C, sew squares together. Weave in all ends.

Applied I-cord Border

With A, cast on 4 sts.

Step 1: K3, sl 1 as if to knit, pick up and knit a st along edge of afghan, pass slipped st over picked up st—4 sts.

Step 2: Slip all 4 sts back to left-hand needle without turning work, draw yarn tightly across back of work to prepare to knit next row.

Rep Steps 1 and 2 all the way around the afghan. Check your work every few rows to ensure that I-cord is evenly applied.

Polka-Dot Bibs

Make baby's meal time a colorful affair with these adorable easy care bibs. They stitch up in a jiffy and you can make a set in several colors for a gorgeous baby shower gift. No one will actually believe you made them yourself.

Difficulty: **Easy**
Finished Measurements: **9" × 9"**
(23cm × 23cm) excluding straps
Fits infants 6-9 months

With A cast on 30 sts and knit 1 row. Mark this row as the Right Side (RS). Working in Garter st, inc 1 st each end of every row six times—42 sts. Work even until 8" (20cm) from beginning, end by working a Wrong Side row.

Divide for Neck/Left Strap

K15, turn and put remaining sts on a holder. Dec 1 st at beginning of next row, then at same edge every row until 9 sts remain. Work even until strap measures approximately 5" (13cm). Dec 1 st at each end of next 2 rows—5 sts.
Bind off.

Right Strap

With RS facing, bind off center 12 sts, K to end. Dec 1 st at end of next row, then at same edge every row until 9 sts remain. Work even until strap measures approximately 5" (13cm). Dec 1 st at each end of next row—7 sts.
Next Row (Buttonhole Row): K2tog, k1, yo, k2tog, k2tog.
Bind off.

Finishing

Edging Rnd 1: With RS facing and crochet hook, join B and work sc evenly around entire outer edge and neck edge, working 3 sc in corners and in the buttonhole space, taking care to keep work flat; join with a sl st to first sc.

Rnd 2: Ch 1, sc in each sc around and 2 sc in each corner st; join. Fasten off. Weave in ends.
Sew button to end of left strap.

Polka Dots

Worked with a crochet hook and your choice of crochet thread colors. Dots are worked in continuous rnds without joining. Mark last st of rnd with a safety pin to indicate end of rnd. Move pin up as each rnd is completed.

Polka-Dot Bibs

Extra-Large Polka Dot

Ch 3; join with a sl st to form a ring.

Rnd 1: 6 Sc in ring; do not join.

Rnd 2: 2 Sc in each sc around—12 sc.

Rnd 3: [Sc in next sc, 2 sc in next sc] six times—18 sc.

Rnd 4: [Sc in next 2 sc, 2 sc in next sc] six times—24 sc.

Rnd 5: [Sc in next 3 sc, 2 sc in next sc] six times—30 sc.

Rnd 6: [Sc in next 4 sc, 2 sc in next sc] six times—36 sc. Remove safety pin, sl st in next 2 sc. Fasten off leaving a long tail for sewing.

Large Polka Dot

Work same as Extra Large Polka Dot through Rnd 5. Remove safety pin, sl st in next 2 sc. Fasten off leaving a long tail for sewing.

Medium Polka Dot

Work same as Extra Large Polka Dot through Rnd 4. Remove safety pin, sl st in next 2 sc. Fasten off leaving a long tail for sewing.

Small Polka Dot

Work same as Extra Large Polka Dot through Rnd 3. Remove safety pin, sl st in next 2 sc. Fasten off leaving a long tail for sewing.

Arrange dots as desired and sew in place.

Garter Stripe
Baby Blanket

Garter Stripe Baby Blanket

Simple garter stripes and artful crossed stitches combine to make this baby blanket a real keeper. Great for all the tiny tots in your family or as a show-stopping gift for a baby shower.

Finished Measurements:
32" wide × 38 ¹/₂" long (81 × 98cm).
Difficulty: **Intermediate**

Materials List

YARN
Red Heart Soft Baby Steps (100% acrylic, 256yd [230m])

- 2 skeins in color 9800 Baby Blue (A)
- 3 skeins in color 9600 White (B)

NEEDLES & NOTIONS
Size US 8 (5mm) 36" (91cm) circular knitting needle

Yarn needle

GAUGE
16 sts and 18 rows = 4" (10cm) in Pat B.

Notes
Blanket is made from side to side.

With A, cast on 154 sts. Knit 5 rows, knit 2 rows B, knit 2 rows A, knit 2 rows B, knit 6 rows A. Now work in patts as follows:

Pattern A
Row 1 (RS): With B, knit.
Row 2 and every WS row: K3, p148, k3.
Rows 3, 7, 11, 15: K5, * yo; k3, pass the first of the 3 knit sts over the 2nd and 3rd sts—3CR (3 Crossed sts) made; repeat from * to last 5 sts; k5.

Rows 5, 9, 13: K4, * 3CR, yo; repeat from * to last 3 sts; k3.
Row 16: Repeat Row 2.

Pattern B
Knit 6 rows A, knit 2 rows B, knit 2 rows A, knit 2 rows B, knit 6 rows A.

Pattern C
Row 1 (RS): With B, knit.
Row 2 and every WS row: K3, p148, k3.
Rows 3, 7, 11, 15: K3, * 3CR, yo; repeat from * to last 3 sts; k3.
Rows 5, 9, 13: K3, * yo, 3CR; repeat from * to last 3 st; k3.
Row 16: Repeat Row 2.
Work Pat B, then Pat A one time, then work [Pat B, Pat C, Pat B, Pat A] twice, then work 12 rows of Pat B; knit 5 rows A. Bind off all sts in knit.

Cuddly Lamb

This adorable knit lamb will be sure to create baby love at first sight. Eight inches (20cm) tall and worked in two colors, it's just the right size for pint-sized hands to hold and hug.

Design by **Barbara Prime**
Finished Measurements: **8" (20cm) tall**
Difficulty: **Intermediate**

Cuddly Lamb

Materials List

YARN

Red Heart Designer Sport (100% acrylic, 279yds [251m])

- 1 skein in color 3101 Ivory (A)
- 1 skein in color 3410 Granite (B)

NEEDLES & NOTIONS

Size US 6 (4mm) knitting needles

Black embroidery thread

Polyester fiberfill

Yarn needle

GAUGE

22 sts and 32 rows = 4" (10cm)

Legs (make 2)

With B, cast on 10 sts.

Purl 1 row.

Row 1: K1, (M1, k1) across—19 sts.

Row 2: Purl.

Row 3: K2, M1, k6, M1, k3, M1, k6, M1, k2—23 sts.

Row 4: Purl.

Cut B and join A.

With A, work 2 rows in St st.

Row 7: K7, SKP twice, k2tog twice, k8—19 sts.

Row 8: P6, p2tog twice, p2tog-tbl twice, p5—15 sts.

Row 9: K6, k2tog, k7—14 sts.

Work 3 rows in St st.

Row 13: K1, M1, k12, M1, k1—16 sts.

Work 9 rows in St st.

Row 23: K1, k2tog seven times, k1—9 sts.

Row 24: Purl.

Row 25: K1, k2tog four times—5 sts.

Cut yarn, leaving a long tail. Thread end through remaining stitches, pull tight to close and knot to secure.

Body

With A and beginning at neck edge, cast on 15 stitches.

Purl 1 row.

Row 1: K1 (m1, k1) across—29 sts.

Work 5 rows in St st.

Row 7: (K7, M1) twice, k1, (M1, k7) twice—33 sts.

Work 5 rows in St st.

Row 13: K15, M1, k3, M1, k15—35 sts.

Work 3 rows in St st.

Row 17: K3, M1, k1, M1, k27, M1, k1, M1, k3—39 sts.

Row 18: Purl.

Row 19: K16, SKP, k3, k2tog, k16—37 sts.

Work 3 rows in St st.

Row 23: K15, SKP, k3, k2tog, k15—35 sts.

Work 3 rows in St st.

Row 27: K1, k2tog seventeen times—18 sts.

Row 28: Purl.

Row 29: K2tog across—9 sts.

Cut yarn, leaving a long tail. Thread end through remaining stitches, pull tight to close and knot to secure.

Right Arm

With B, cast on 6 stitches.

Purl 1 row.

Row 1: K1, (M1, k1) across—11 sts.

Row 2: Purl.

Row 3: (K2, M1) twice, k3, (M1, k2) twice—15 sts.

Row 4: Purl.

Cut B and join A.

With A, work 2 rows in St st.

Row 7: K1, SKP twice, k2tog twice, k6—11 sts.

Work 3 rows in St st.

Row 11: K1, M1, k9, M1, k1—13 sts.

Work 9 rows in St st.

Row 21: K1, k2tog six times—7 sts.

Row 22: Purl.

Row 23: K1, (k2tog, k1) twice—5 sts.

Cut yarn, leaving a long tail. Thread end through remaining stitches, pull tight to close and knot to secure.

Left Arm

With B, cast on 6 stitches.

Purl 1 row.

Row 1: K1, (M1, k1) across—11 sts.

Row 2: Purl.

Row 3: (K2, M1) twice, k3, (M1, k2) twice—15 sts.

Row 4: Purl.

Cut B and join A.

With A, work 2 rows in St st.

Row 7: K6, SKP twice, k2tog twice, k1—11 sts.

Continue to work remaining rows as for Right Arm.

Head

With A, cast on 7 sts.

Purl 1 row.

Row 1: K1, (M1, k1) across—13 sts.

Row 2: Purl.

Row 3: K1, (M1, k1) across—25 sts.

Work 3 rows in St st.

Row 7: K1, (M1, k3) across—33 sts.

Work 10 rows in St st.

Cut A and join B.

Row 26: With B, purl 1 row.

Row 27: K12, k2tog, k5, SKP, k12—31 sts.

Row 28: Purl.

Row 29: K2tog seven times, k3, SKP seven times—17 sts.

Work 3 rows in St st.

Row 33: K1, (k2tog) across—9 sts.

Cut yarn, leaving a long tail. Thread end through remaining stitches, pull tight to close and knot to secure.

Ears (make 2)

With A, cast on 4 sts.

Row 1: Knit.

Row 2: K1, M1, k to last st, M1, k1.

Repeat last 2 rows once more—10 sts.

Work in garter stitch for 8 rows.

Bind off.

Tail

With A, cast on 8 sts.

Beginning with a WS row, work 5 rows in St st.

Next Row: K2tog four times—4 sts.

Cut yarn, leaving a long tail. Thread end through remaining stitches, pull tight to close and knot to secure.

Finishing

Embroider face on Head with straight stitches. Stuff Head tightly with fiberfill, adding extra fiberfill in nose area and sew closed. Fold bound-off edge of each Ear in half and sew together. Sew bound-off edge of each Ear on either side of Head. Sew up back seam of Body to neck edge, leaving neck edge open. Stuff tightly. Sew Head securely to open neck edge of Body.

Sew seam of each Arm, leaving an opening. Stuff tightly and sew closed. Thread a length of yarn through Left Arm about 1/4" (6mm) from top edge, pull yarn through Body at shoulder position, then thread yarn though Right Arm. Pull yarn through Body again, and then through Left Arm, pulling tightly. Repeat several times so Arms are in place securely. Sew sole and back Leg seams, leaving an opening for stuffing. Stuff tightly with fiberfill and sew closed. Attach Legs at lower edge of Body in same manner as Arms.

Sew tail in place. Weave in ends.

Accessories

When we sit down to come up with ideas for each episode of the TV show, we usually break pattern options down into categories, and accessories is always at the top of that list. Whether it's scarves or gloves, hats or bags, accessories are fun and usually fast to make. We have pulled together a group of wonderful projects that range from easy to intermediate and from subtle to colorful; there is something for everyone. This is one category that is sure to please.

Braided Scarf

Creative I-cord braids make this unique scarf a must have. This is the perfect whip-it-up-quick project on big needles. The finished scarf looks like you spent days and days making it.

*Design by **Susan B. Anderson** for Spud & Chloë*
*Finished Measurements: **4 ¹/₂" (11cm) wide on the rib sections, 2 ¹/₄" (6cm) wide on the braid sections, 76" (193cm) long***
*Difficulty: **Intermediate***

Materials List

YARN

3 skeins Spud & Chloë Outer (65% superwash wool, 35% organic cotton, 60yd [54m]) in color 7200 Soapstone

NEEDLES & NOTIONS

Size US 17 (12.75mm) needles

Set of 4 size US 13 (9mm) double-pointed needles (dpns)

Yarn needle

Scissors

Tape measure or ruler

GAUGE

1 ³/₄ sts = 1" (3cm) in Stockinette stitch

Notes

You can make the scarf any length desired. Just bind off at the end of a Rib Section.

Rib Section

With the larger size needles cast on 15 stitches.

Row 1: (K1, p1) repeat to end.

Row 2: (P1, k1) repeat to end.

Repeat Rows 1 and 2 until the ribbed section measures 6" (15cm) ending with a Row 2.

Braid Section

Using two dpns to work in I-cord, knit first 5 stitches onto one dpn, leaving the remaining stitches on the larger needle. Work the 5 stitches in I-cord until the cord measures 6" (10cm). Cut the yarn, leaving a 4" (10cm) end leaving the stitches on the dpn.

Reattach the yarn leaving a 4" (10cm) tail to begin working on the next 5 stitches. Knit the middle 5 stitches. Repeat the I-cord as for the first cord including cutting the yarn and leaving the stitches on the needle. Reattach the yarn leaving a 4" (10cm) tail and knit the last 5 stitches. Repeat the third I-cord as for the first and second I-cord. For this cord leave the yarn attached. Now you have three 6" (15cm) I-cords on three separate dpns. The cord on the left has the working yarn still attached. Starting with the left I-cord, braid the cords together until the cord with the attached yarn ends up on the Right Side.

Finishing

Work back onto the larger needles directly from the dpns holding the stitches. Continue repeating the Rib Section and Braid Section until you reach the desired length. End the scarf with a Rib Section.

Bind off, cut the yarn and pull through the remaining stitches. With a yarn needle, weave in and trim all ends from the cast on, I-cords and bound-off edge.

Earflap Hat

Warm and practical, colorful and playful, this earflap hat takes a practical accessory and makes it fashionable. It is knit in a traditional pattern but with bold colors that are anything but old-fashioned.

*Design by **Jenn Jarvis***
*Finished Measurements: **17 ¹/₂" circ.***
Hat fits most women.
*Difficulty: **Intermediate***

Materials List

YARN

Red Heart Super Saver (100% acrylic, 364 yds [328])

- 1 skein in color 0656 Real Teal (A)
- 1 skein in color 319 Cherry Red (B)
- 1 skein in color 0657 Dusty Teal (C)

NEEDLES & NOTIONS

Size US 8 (5mm) double-pointed needles (dpns)

Size US 8 (5mm) 16" (41cm) circular knitting needle

Size US J/10 (6mm) crochet hook

Stitch marker

Yarn needle

Pom-pom maker

GAUGE

17 sts and 20 rows = 4" (10cm) in Fair Isle pattern

Notes

Carry color not in use loosely across Wrong Side of work. When changing colors, pick up new color to be used under color just used to prevent a hole.

Earflap (Make 2)

With C, cast on 3 sts using dpns.

Row 1 (RS): Knit.

Row 2 and all even rows: Purl.

Row 3: K1, [M1, k1] twice—5 sts.

Row 5: K1, M1, k3, M1, k1—7 sts.

Row 7: K1, M1, k5, M1, k1—9 sts.

Row 9: K1, M1, k7, M1, k1—11 sts.

Row 11: K1, M1, k9, M1, k1—13 sts.

Row 13: K1, M1, k11, M1, k1—15 sts.

Row 14: Purl.

[Knit 1 row, purl 1 row] twice. Do not bind off.

Hat

With circular needle, cast on 10 sts. With RS facing, knit across 15 sts of one Earflap, turn, cast on 25 sts, turn. With RS facing, knit across 15 sts of remaining Earflap, turn, cast on 10 sts. Join to work in the round placing a stitch marker between first and last sts to mark beginning/end of rnds—75 sts.

Earflap Hat

Knit 2 rnds even. Now work Rows 1–31 from chart on page 37. Cut A and B. Continue with C only until hat measures 7" (18cm) from beginning. Change to dpns while working next rnd, dividing sts onto three needles.

Shape Top
Next Rnd: [K2tog] thirty-seven times, k1—38 sts.
Next 2 Rnds: Knit.
Next Rnd: [K2tog] nineteen times—19 sts.
Next 2 Rnds: Knit.
Next Rnd: [K2tog] nine times, k1—10 sts.
Cut yarn and weave tail through remaining sts; draw up firmly, secure on WS.

Finishing
With RS facing and crochet hook, attach A at center back; ch 1, sc around lower edge of Hat, including Earflaps, taking care to keep work flat; join with a slip st in first sc. Fasten off.

Tie
Cut nine 30" (76cm) strands of A and draw through sts at point of Earflap to the midpoint of the strands. Divide the lengths into three sections of six strands each and braid them for 11" (28cm). Knot the end of the braid. Trim ends even. Repeat for other Earflap.

Using pom-pom maker and A, make one 3" (8cm) pom-pom and secure to top of Hat.

Fair Isle Chart

Fingerless Gloves with Embroidery

Keep your hands toasty and your fingers free to work, or knit, in these colorful embellished gloves. Simple stripes, lazy daisy embroidery and a picot edge make this project a real standout.

*Design by **Kristin Nicholas***
*Finished Measurements: **Child's medium (6" [15cm] in circumference), Child's large/ Woman's small (7" [18cm] in circumference), Woman's large/Man's small (8" [20cm] in circumference), Man's large (9" [23cm] in circumference)***
*Difficulty: **Intermediate***

Materials List

YARN
Nashua Handknits Julia (50% wool, 25% mohair, 25% alpaca, 93yd [84m])
- 1 ball in color NHJ4936 Blue Thyme (A)
- 1 ball in color NHJ2163 Golden Honey (B)
- 1 ball in color NHJ0178 Harvest Spice (C)

NEEDLES & NOTIONS
Set of 4 size US 7 (4.5mm) double-pointed needles (dpns)

Set of 4 size US 6 (4 mm) dpns

Tapestry needle

Stitch markers

Stitch holders

GAUGE
20 sts and 26 rounds = 4" (10cm) in Stockinette stitch worked in the round using larger needle

Notes
Bobble Edging
*P3, (k1, p1, k1, p1) all in same stitch to increase 1 stitch to 4 stitches, turn work so Wrong Side is facing, k4 bobble stitches, turn work so Right Side is facing, P4 bobble stitches, pass 2nd, 3rd, and 4th stitches on right needle over first stitch to decrease bobble back to 1 stitch; repeat from * to end of round.

Garter Ridge
Rnd 1: Knit.
Rnd 2: Purl.

2 × 2 Corrugated Rib
Set-up Rnd: *K2 with B, k2 with C; repeat from * to end.
All other Rnds: *K2 with B, bring C to front of work, p2 with C, bring C to back of work; repeat from * to end. Repeat last rnd only for pattern; do not repeat the Set-up Rnd.

Stockinette Stitch in the round
Knit all stitches every round.

Knitting the Cuff
Using A, CO 28 (32, 40, 44) sts. Divide stitches as evenly as possible on three needles. Place marker and join for working in the round, being careful not to twist stitches.

Next Rnd: Work 1 round for Bobble Edging.

Next 2 Rnds: Work 1 Garter Ridge.

Change to B and C and work in 2 × 2 Corrugated Rib for 2 1/4 (2 1/2, 3, 3 1/4) [6 (6, 8, 8)cm] inches.

Next 2 Rnds: Change to A and work 1 Garter Ridge.

Change to larger needles and cont in A for rem of glove in St st.

In Rnd 1, inc evenly 2 (4, 0, 2) sts to give 30 (36, 40, 46) sts.

Work even in Stockinette stitch for one (two, three, four) more rounds.

Beg Thumb Gusset

Rnd 1: K 15 (18, 20, 23) sts, place marker for Thumb Gusset, M1, place marker for Thumb Gusset; knit rem 15 (18, 20, 23) sts—31 (37, 41, 47) sts.

You now have 1 stitch between the gusset markers for all sizes.

Rnd 2: Knit 1 rnd even for all sizes.

Rnd 3 (increase rnd): Knit to first Thumb Gusset marker, slip marker, M1, knit to second Thumb Gusset marker, M1, slip marker, knit to end: 2 stitches increased between gusset markers.

Repeat the last 2 rnds 4 (5, 6, 7) more times—41 (49, 55, 63) sts with 11 (13, 15, 17) sts bet gusset markers

Next Rnd: Knit to first gusset marker, remove marker, place gusset stitches on holder, remove second gusset marker, knit to end—30 (36, 40, 46) sts.

Work even in Stockinette stitch until Glove reaches base of pinky finger, or until Stockinette section measures above last Garter Ridge about 3 1/2 (4, 4 1/2, 5) inches [9 (10, 11, 13)cm].

Next 2 Rnds: Change to B and work 1 Garter Ridge.

Next Rnd: Change to C.

Child's medium only: *K4, k2tog; repeat from * to end.

Child's large/Woman's small only: *K4, k2tog; repeat from * to end.

Woman's large/Man's small only: *K4, k2tog; repeat from * to last 4 stitches, k4.

Man's large only: *K4, k2tog; repeat from * to last 4 stitches, k4—25 (30, 34, 39) sts.

Next Rnd: Purl.

Bind off all sts in C.

Thumb

Place held stitches from Thumb Gusset on two needles. Join C to beginning of thumb stitches with Right Side facing. Knit across thumb stitches, then pick up and knit 1 stitch from base of hole where hand stitches rejoined for working in the round—12 (14, 16, 18) sts.

Divide stitches as evenly as possible among three needles.

Rnds 2-3: Change to B and work 1 Garter Ridge.

Rnd 4: Change to C.

Child's medium only: *K3, k2tog; repeat from * to last 2 stitches, k2.

Child's large/Woman's small only: *K3, k2tog; repeat from * to last 4 stitches, k4.

Woman's large/Man's small only: *K3, k2tog; repeat from * to last stitch, k1.

Man's large only: *K3, k2tog; repeat from * to last 3 stitches, k3.

You now have 10 (12, 13, 15) sts.

Next Rnd: Purl.

Bind off all stitches neatly.

Finishing

Weave in ends. Use the yarn tail at base of Thumb to close up any remaining holes where the Thumb meets the hand.

Note: Make sure to work embroidery on the opposite side for each Glove so you will have both a right and left hand.

Embroidery

Using a single strand of B, embroider 3 or 4 lazy daisy flowers on the back of each Glove as shown in photo. With a single strand of C, embroider French knots in the center of each daisy flower. Weave in ends.

French Knot

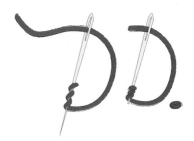

To make a French knot, bring needle up through material, wrap thread around tip of needle the desired number of times, thrust needle downward 1 or 2 threads from where it was brought up. Draw thread through carefully to from knot on RS. Bring needle up in position for next French knot.

Lazy Daisy Stitch

1 *Bring needle up at inner point of petal, hold thread toward you. Push needle down through fabric at inner point of petal, 1 or 2 threads to right of point where thread emerges.*

2 *Bring point of needle out at outer end of petal, going over thread.*

3 *Draw loop toward you to form petal, push needle down through fabric outside of loop to fasten in place.*

Butterfly Wallet

Keep all your makeup needs right in one place with this beautiful butterfly bag. Knit up the bag and the butterfly in colorful wool then just felt for added strength. The zipper close on the top keeps everything safely inside.

Design by **Maggie Pace**
Finished Measurements: *7" × 6"*
(18cm × 15cm)
Difficulty: **Easy**

Notes

Short Row shaping: When working St st, a Short Row is created by turning the work (TW) partway through a knit row, working in purl the number of stitches indicated, turning the work again and working in knit the number of stitches indicated. One short row can have several turns.

Knit the Wallet

Using A, cast on 29 sts.

Row 1 (RS): Knit.

Row 2: Purl.

Rows 3-4: Rep Rows 1 and 2.

Row 5: K14, inc in the next st, k14—30 sts.

Row 6: Purl.

Row 7: K15, inc in next st, k14—31 sts.

Row 8: Purl.

Row 9: K15, inc in next st, k15—32 sts.

Row 10: Purl.

Rows 11-70: Work in St st.

Row 71: Knit.

Row 72: Purl.

Row 73: K15, k2tog, k15—31 sts.

Row 74: Purl.

Row 75: K14, k2tog, k15—30 sts.

Row 76: Purl.

Row 77: K14, k2tog, k14—29 sts.

Row 78: Purl.

Row 79: Knit.

Row 80: Purl.

Bind off all sts. Weave in ends.

Seam the Wallet

Fold piece in half with Wrong Sides together so the cast-on and bound-off edges meet. Using a yarn needle threaded with A, sew side seams.

Knit Butterfly Embellishment

The wings are made using Short Rows.

Work Right Wing

Using B, CO 9 sts.

Row 1 (a Short Row):

*K3 and TW

P3 and TW

Butterfly Wallet

K4 and TW
P4 and TW
K5 and TW
P5 and TW
K6 and TW
P6 and TW
K7 and TW
P7 and TW
K8 and TW
Purl to end. *

Row 2: Still using B, cast on 9 sts to the same needle holding the 9 sts just worked—18 sts.
Repeat pattern between *s.

Row 3: K2tog nine times—9 sts.
Row 4: P2tog. *P2tog. Lift first st on right-hand needle over the second st and off the needle to bind off.*
Repeat between *s until all sts are bound off. Cut B and fasten off stitch. Weave in all ends.

Work Left Wing

Repeat Right Wing pattern except knit all purls and purl all knits.

Finishing

Using B threaded in a yarn needle, join the Left and Right Wings at the bound-off edges: Arrange so the Wings are side by side, RS facing up and bound-off edges touching. Send needle under both loops of the first bound-off stitches on each Wing. Return in the opposite direction. Continue weaving the seam in this manner until the two Wings are joined. Weave in ends.

Felting

1. Set the machine to hot and on the lowest water, highest agitation cycle. Start the washing machine. Let the basin fill with hot water.
2. When the agitator starts moving, add the Wallet and Butterfly Embellishment to the water.
3. Check for doneness. It will take a few minutes for your items to show signs of shrinkage. Once they do, check often, at least every 1 or 2 minutes. If the agitation cycle is done and the items still aren't felted, manually reset your machine to go through the agitation cycle again without letting it go through the spin cycle. You may need to felt the Wallet longer than the Butterfly (or vice versa) to get the desired proportion.

Your items are done when:
   - The stitch definition has disappeared.
   - They are stiff to the touch.
   - The Wallet measures about 7" (18cm) across the top and the Butterfly Embellishment is in good proportion to the Wallet.

4. When you've determined the Wallet and Butterfly Embellishment are finished, rinse in the sink and squeeze out excess water by hand.

Blocking

Block Wallet so that it squares off. Press butterfly flat. Let items dry flat.

Decorate Butterfly Embellishment
French Knots

Begin by adding French knots (see page 41) to Butterfly Embellishment. Position the knots as shown in the photo.

Blanket Stitch Edging

Thread a yarn needle with A and blanket stitch around the edge of the wallet.

Running & Overcast Stitch

Thread a yarn needle with C and apply a running stitch (see page 17) on both Wings as shown in project photo. Wrap the butterfly's body with an overcast stitch.

Apply the Butterfly Embellishment

Next sew the Butterfly Embellishement onto the Wallet using a yarn needle threaded with B. As you sew, don't pass the needle all the way through the Butterfly Embellishment or the Wallet—just catch enough of both fabrics to secure the Butterfly Embellishment to the Wallet.

Sew In Zipper

1. Open Zipper. With the Wallet Right Side out, pin the Zipper against the top inside opening with the Zipper head against one corner, the top stop at the outer corner and Zipper teeth just clear of the Wallet edge.

2. Turn the Wallet inside out. Using a matching sewing thread doubled, sew from the top stop to the Zipper head with a backstitch. Sew as close to the Wallet edge as possible. Remove pins as you progress.

3. Use an overcast stitch to tack the unsewn edges of the Zipper to the Wallet's interior. At the top stop, turn the unsewn ends at a downward angle and tack.

Blanket Stitch

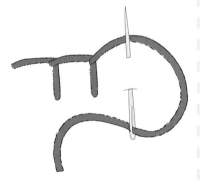

Working from left to right, draw thread through at desired distance from edge. Hold thread at left and toward you. Push needle down through fabric at desired spot and draw toward you, passing over thread. Draw up until a line of thread lies along the edge. Keep stitches evenly spaced.

Backstitch

Take a small running stitch (see page 17), insert needle at end of running stitch, thrust needle through to Wrong Side and over twice as much space as original stitch on Wrong Side; bring needle to Right Side and repeat.

Overcast Stitch

Bring the needle up through the fabric on one side near the edge of the piece, then bring the needle and thread over and around the edge of the fabric and through again a little beyond the last stitch. The overcast stitch is the same as the familiar whipstitch only whipstitch is worked to attach two pieces of fabric.

Bloom Loom Scarf

No need to wait for spring to wrap yourself in a garden of flowers. Just stitch up this charming, blooming scarf. Made with a Bloom Loom, the flowers work up fast and then you just stitch them together.

Design by **Candi Jensen**
Finished Measurements: **6" × 60"**
(15cm × 152cm)
Difficulty: **Easy**

Materials List

YARN
Worsted weight cotton or cotton blend ribbon in your choice of colors

Novelty eyelash yarn in your choice of colors

NEEDLES & NOTIONS
Size US H/8 (5mm) crochet hook

Boye Bloom Loom

Large eye yarn needle

Make 32 flowers according to the instructions in the Bloom Loom. You might want to practice using leftover yarn before you begin with the scarf. For best results use the colors randomly throughout. You can join the flowers while working as indicated in the Bloom Loom instructions or sew them together once you have finished all 32 flowers.

Finishing

Once you have finished the flowers sew them together in 16 rows of 2 flowers each. Join 2 petals on each side of flowers to adjoining petals of previous flowers, always leaving one petal free between joinings. Finishing: Once you have sewn the flowers together, use the crochet hook to join the light pink ribbon to the side loops of a flower. Work an sc, ch 3, sc in next group of loops; cont in this manner around the scarf.

Infinity Scarf

Part scarf, part shawl, this is the perfect multi-purpose piece to keep you warm and fashionable. Quick and easy to knit using two strands of yarn and big needles, you will be able to make this scarf in a different color for every occasion.

Design by **Candi Jensen**
Finished Measurements: **15" × 34"
(38cm × 86cm)**
Difficulty: **Easy**

Materials List

YARN

3 skeins Caron Country (75% microdenier Acrylic, 25% Merino Wool, 185yd [167m]) in color 0012 Foliage

NEEDLES & NOTIONS

Size US 13 (9mm) needles

Large eye yarn needle

GAUGE

12 sts and 12 rows= 4" (10cm)

Notes
Pattern Stitch

Rows 1, 2, 3: Knit.

Row 4: Purl.

Repeat these 4 rows for pattern.

Cast on 102 sts very loosely (use 1 large and 1 small needle held together if need be). Begin pattern st. Work in pattern st until piece measures 15" (38cm), ending with the bind off on Row 4.

Finishing

Sew ends together so it makes a circle.

Men's Sampler Scarf

This clever sampler scarf is sure to be a hit with the guys and is a perfect way to spruce up your skills. It's worked in five different pattern stitches and a variety of yarn colors for a one-of-a-kind look.

Design by **Drew Emborsky**
Finished Measurements: **7" × 75"**
(18cm × 191cm)
Difficulty: **Easy**

Materials List

YARN
Red Heart Collage (100% acrylic, 155yds [140m])

- 1 skein in color 2930 Karma
- 1 skein in color 2940 Blue Moon
- 1 skein in color 2945 Sedona
- 1 skein in color 2950 Forest
- 1 skein in color 2955 Glad

NEEDLES & NOTIONS
Size US 9 (5.5mm) needles

Cable needle

Yarn needle

GAUGE
16 sts and 21 rows = 4" (10cm) in Stockinette st.

Pattern Stitches

Cable 2 front (C2F): Place next 2 sts on cable needle and hold in front, knit next 2 sts, then knit sts from cable needle.

Panel A (Make 2)

Make 1 in Sedona and 1 in Glade.

Cast on 21 sts.

Rows 1–4: Knit.

Row 5: K3, p15, k3.

Row 6: Knit.

Rows 7–18: Repeat Rows 5–6.

Rows 19–21: Knit.

Bind off.

Panel B (Make 2)

Make 1 in Forest and 1 in Blue Moon

Cast on 7 sts.

Row 1: K1, [p1, k1] three times.

Row 2: P1, [k1, p1] three times.

Rows 3–78: Repeat Rows 1 and 2.

Bind off.

Panel C (Make 2)

Make 1 in Sedona and 1 in Forest.

Cast on 14 sts.

Rows 1–4: Knit.

Row 5: K5, p4, k5.

Row 6: K3, p2, k4, p2, k3.

Row 7: K5, p4, k5.

Row 8: K3, p2, C2F, p2, k3.

Rows 9–87: Repeat Rows 5–8 ending with a Row 7.

Rows 88–90: Knit.

Bind off.

Panel D (Make 2)

Make 1 in Blue Moon and 1 in Glade.

Cast on 100 sts.

Row 1: * K2, p2; repeat from * across.

Row 2: * P2, k2; repeat from * across.

Rows 3–8: Repeat Rows 1 and 2.

Bind off in pattern.

Panel E (Make 2)

Make 1 in Glade and 1 in Sedona.

Cast on 20 sts.

Rows 1–51: Knit.

Bind off.

Assembly

Lay out panels according to diagram and whipstitch together to create two halves of Scarf. Line up each half of Scarf with Panels B and E in center and whipstitch together. Weave in all ends.

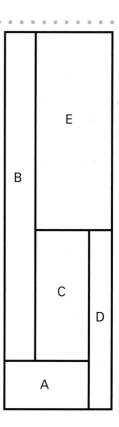

Construction Diagram

Home Decor

We receive a lot of positive feedback from our viewers, and they are always very enthusiastic about our projects for the home. In fact the Afghan Square of the Week is our most popular project, and it's easy to see why. You can work your way through a number of different stitch techniques from easy to intermediate, and when you're done, you have a lovely afghan. However, we not only feature afghans but colorful pillows, a chair cushion, dishcloths and even a recycled T-shirt rug. I'm sure you'll find something for every room in your house.

Pillow with Garter Ridges and Embroidery

Sure to warm up any room, this colorful pillow may look difficult but is made with very basic stitches. Worked in stripes of Garter ridges, the trick is in the finishing embellishments.

Design by **Kristin Nicholas**
Finished Measurements:
13" (33cm) square
Difficulty: **Easy**

Materials List

YARN

Nashua Handknits Julia (50% Wool, 25% Alpaca, 25% Mohair, 93yd [84m])

- 2 skeins in color NHJ3158 Purple Basil (A)
- 1 skein in color NHJ3961 Lady's Mantle (B)
- 1 skein in Gourd NHJ1784 (C)

Small amount of scrap yarn

NEEDLES & NOTIONS

Size US 7 (4.5mm) 29" (174cm) circular needle

Size US 9 (5.5mm) 29" (74cm) circular needle

Size G/6 (4mm) crochet hook

Tapestry needle

Polyester fiberfill or 14" (36cm) down pillow form to fit

1/2yd (45cm) backing fabric

Sewing thread and needle

GAUGE

18 sts = 4" (10cm) on larger needles in Stockinette st

Notes

Because Garter stitch stretches laterally and produces a different gauge than Stockinette stitch, the Garter ridges are worked on a needle one size smaller than the Stockinette stitch sections.

Pattern Stitches

Stockinette Stitch (back and forth):
Row 1: (RS) Knit all sts.
Row 2: (WS) Purl all sts.

Garter Ridge (back and forth):
Row 1: (RS) Knit all sts.
Row 2: (WS) Knit all sts.

Garter Ridge (in the round for mitered trim)
Rnd 1: (RS) Knit all sts.
Rnd 2: (RS) Purl all sts.

Provisional Cast-On

With crochet hook, chain 50 sts with scrap yarn. Using circular needle, with A, pick up 50 sts through the

Pillow with Garter Ridges and Embroidery

"bump" on the chain. This is called a provisional cast-on. Work 11 rows of Stockinette stitch beg with a WS Row. [* Using smaller circular needle, work a Garter Ridge in B. Work a Garter Ridge in A. * Repeat bet *'s once more. Work a Garter Ridge in Color B Lady's Mantle. You will have a total of 5 Garter Ridges. Change to larger needle and work 12 rows using A in Stockinette st.] Remember to use the smaller needle for the Garter Ridge sections and the larger needle for the Stockinette st sections.

Repeat between [ ]'s twice more. You should have a total of 4 Color A stripes and 3 Garter Ridge Stripes. Do not bind off.

Mitered Edge

Pick up sts all the way around the four sides using the smaller circular needle. Work several Garter Ridges, increasing 2 sts at each corner every other round.

 * Using the smaller circular needle and B with RS facing, * knit 50 sts from pillow, place marker (pm), pick up 1 st in corner, pm, pick up and knit 47 sts along selvedge edge, pm, pick up 1 st in corner, pm. Remove the provisional-CO sts and knit these 50 sts. Undo the last loop on the crochet and unravel the stitches so they are live. Pick up and knit the 50 live sts with the circular needle and color you are working with, pm, pick up 1 st in corner, pm, pick up and knit 47 sts along remaining selvedge edge, pm, pick up 1 st in corner, pm. Work Garter Ridges in the round to form the mitered border.

Always knit the marked corner stitch on each round. This gives a definite mitered line to each corner. (The pick-up round in the first Garter Ridge counts as Round 1.)

Rnd 2: Purl one round, knitting each corner st, and increasing 1 st on both sides of each corner st as follows: *Work to marker (m), increase 1 st before the m by placing a backward loop on the needle (referred to as M1), sl m, k1 (corner st), sl m, M1; repeat from * to end of round—8 sts increased.

Change to A and knit one round.
Repeat Rnd 2 above to increase 8 sts and continue the mitered corners.

Work a second Garter Ridge in B increasing on second round.
Work a second Garter Ridge in A increasing on second round.
Work a third Garter Ridge in B increasing on second round.
Bind off all sts in B.

Embroidery

Using C, thread the tapestry needle with a double strand. In the second row on each side of the Garter Ridge stripes, work in running stitch (see page 17) over and under every stitch to create small dots. Pull on the stitching to release and make the embroidery stitches relax. Work this running stitch on either side of each stripe as shown in photo. Weave in ends.

Block the Pillow Top

Using a spray bottle, thoroughly mist the pillow top with warm water. With your hands, work the water into the knitted fabric. Using large T-pins, pin out the fabric on a flat padded surface (like an unused bed). Using a steam iron and holding the iron 2" (5cm) away from the fabric, steam lightly. Avoid touching the pillow with the iron or the fabric may become flattened or scorched. Leave to

dry. Alternately, handwash pillow top in cold water with
a cold rinse and lay flat to dry.

Cut a piece of fabric 1" (3cm) wider and longer than the
pillow top. Turn under $1/2$" (1cm) all around and press.
Hand stitch the pillow top to the fabric around three
sides. Insert the pillow form. Sew the last side closed.

Stained Glass Afghan

Inspired by the afghans that graced the beds during a family retreat, this pattern mimics a stained glass window. Worked in colorful Garter stitch hexagons and bordered in black, this lovely afghan will soon become a family heirloom in your home, too.

Design by **Susan Levin**
Finished Measurements: **52" × 72"**
(132 × 183cm)
Difficulty: **Easy**

Materials List

YARN

Red Heart Classic (100% acrylic, 190yd [171m])

- 2 skeins in color 760 New Berry (A)
- 2 skeins in color 286 Bronze (B)
- 2 skeins in color 339 Mid Brown (C)
- 2 skeins in color 686 Paddy Green (D)
- 2 skeins in color 683 Lt. Seafoam (E)
- 2 skeins in color 848 Skipper Blue (F)
- 2 skeins in color 596 Purple (G)
- 2 skeins in color 401 Nickel (H)
- 3 skeins in color 012 Black (Trim)

NEEDLES & NOTIONS

Size US 8 (5mm) needles

Tapestry needle

Size I/9 (5.5mm) crochet hook (Optional)

GAUGE

19 sts and 36 rows = 4" (10cm) in Garter st.
Gauge is not critical for this project.

Large Diamonds

Make eleven of each color.

CO 3 sts.

Rows 1–16: Knit, increasing 1 st at the beg of each row—19 sts.

Rows 17–64: Knit.

Rows 65–80: K2tog at the beg of each row—3 sts rem.

Row 81: K3tog. BO.

Small Diamonds

Make eight each of colors 4, 5; make nine each of all other colors.

Work as for Large Diamonds until 17 sts. K2tog at the beg of next 14 rows—3 sts.

K3tog.

Bind off.

Half Diamonds

Make one each of colors C, F; make two each of all other colors.

Work as for Large Diamonds until 17 sts.

Bind off.

Stained Glass Afghan

Finish Squares (Crochet Version)

With trim color sc around edge of each diamond, working 3 sc into top and bottom points of Large Diamonds and in each point of Small and Half Diamonds. Whipstitch diamonds together following schematic for placement (page 61).

Finish Squares (Stitching Version)

With two strands of trim color held together, work blanket stitch (see page 45) around edge of each diamond working one stitch in each point. Whipstitch diamonds together following schematic for placement (page 61).

Trim Panels (make 2)

With trim color, work Rows 1–16 as for Large Diamonds, then knit even to fit along straight side when slightly stretched. Work decrease Rows 65–81 as for Large Diamonds.

Finishing

Whipstitch trim panels to body. Along top and bottom borders only work either two rows of sc or one row of buttonhole stitch. For crochet version, work 3 stitches in the valley of each point and 3 stitches in peak of each point. For stitching version, work one stitch in each point and valley. Weave in all ends. Steam lightly.

1	2	3	4	5	6	7	8	1	2	3
6	7	8	1	2	3	4	5	6	7	8	1
4	5	6	7	8	1	2	3	4	5	6
1	2	3	4	5	6	7	8	1	2	3	4
7	8	1	2	3	4	5	6	7	8	1
4	5	6	7	8	1	2	3	4	5	6	7
2	3	4	5	6	7	8	1	2	3	4
7	8	1	2	3	4	5	6	7	8	1	2
5	6	4	7	8	1	2	3	4	5	6
2	3	4	5	6	7	8	1	2	3	4	5
8	1	2	3	4	5	6	7	8	1	2
5	6	7	8	1	2	3	4	5	6	7	8
3	4	5	6	7	8	1	2	3	4	5
8	1	2	3	4	5	6	7	8	1	2	3
6	7	8	1	2	3	4	5	6	7	8

Apple Dishcloth

So cute and oh so practical, this hardworking dishcloth will spruce up your kitchen with its bright and cheery style, but make no mistake—it's up to the challenge of all those cleaning needs. Make them in an array of apple-bright colors!

Design by **Susan B. Anderson**
Finished Measurements: *7 1/4"
(18cm) tall × 6 1/4" (16cm) wide*
Difficulty: **Easy**

Materials List

YARN

Crystal Palace Cotton Chenille (100% combed cotton, 98yd [88m])

• 1 skein in color 9784 Lacquer Red (A)

• 1 skein in color 2342 Fern (B)

Small amount in color 517 Christmas Green (C)

Small amount in color 516 Cocoa (D)

(Optional: Stem can also be done in the same green used for the leaf.)

NEEDLES & NOTIONS

Size G/6 (4mm) crochet hook (Optional: for slip stitch edging only)

Scissors

Ruler or tape measure

Yarn needle

Stitch holder

GAUGE

4 stitches = 1" (3cm) in Stockinette stitch

Apple

With A cast on 20 stitches.

Row 1: K1, kfb, knit to the last 2 stitches, kfb, k1—22 sts.

Row 2: Knit.

Repeat Rows 1 and 2 until there are 32 stitches.

Work even, knitting every row until the Apple measures 4 1/2" (11cm) from the cast-on edge.

Repeat Rows 1 and 2 two more times—36 sts.

Continue knitting every row until the Apple measures 5" (13cm) from the cast-on edge.

Decrease Rows

Row 1: K1, SSK, knit to the last 3 sts, k2tog, k1—34 sts.

Row 2: Knit.

Repeat Rows 1 and 2 two more times—30 sts.

Top of Apple

Next Row: K15, place remaining 15 stitches on a stitch holder, turn and knit to the end of the row.

Decrease Row: K1, SSK, knit to the last 3 stitches, k2tog, k1.

Repeat the decrease row every row until there are 7 stitches remaining.

Bind off.

Reattach the yarn in the middle and return the 15 stitches on the stitch holder back onto the needle. Knit to the end of the row. Complete the same as for the first half of the Top of the Apple.

Apple Dishcloth

Stem

With D or C, pick up 3 stitches in the dip between the top sections of the Apple. Knit every row until the stem measures 1" (3cm). Bind off. Cut the yarn and pull through the remaining stitch.

Leaf

With B cast on 3 stitches.

Row 1: Kfb, knit to last stitch, kfb—5 sts.

Row 2: Knit.

Row 3: Rep Row 1—7 sts.

Rows 4–6: Knit.

Row 7: K1, SSK, k1, k2tog, k1—5 sts.

Row 8: Knit.

Row 9: K1, SSK, k2—4 sts.

Row 10: Knit.

Row 11: SSK, k2tog, pass first stitch over the second stitch and off the right needle—1 st.

Cut the yarn leaving a 6" (15cm) end. Pull the end through the remaining stitch. Place the end on a yarn needle and whipstitch the Leaf to the front of the Apple at the bottom of the Stem. Use the photo as a guide. Pull the end to the Wrong Side of the Leaf and trim.

Optional Crochet Edging

With A and the crochet hook and starting at the left side of the Stem, slip stitch around the edge of the Apple. End at the right side of the Stem. Cut the yarn and pull through the stitch.

Colorwork Pillow

Colorwork Pillow

Give your chair a creative boost with this colorful cushion made with a variety of bright embellishments. Work the cushion in a simple Fair Isle pattern, then make it fabulous with lazy daisy flowers. Perfect for honing your color changing skills.

*Design by **Kristin Nicholas***
*Finished Measurements: **16" × 16"***
(41cm × 41cm)
*Difficulty: **Intermediate***

Materials List

YARN

Nashua Handknits Julia (50% Wool, 25% Alpaca, 25% Mohair, 93yd [84m])
- 1 skein in color NHJ2230 Rock Henna (A)
- 1 skein in color NHJ4936 Blue Thyme (B)
- 1 skein in color NHJ2163 Golden Honey (C)
- 1 skein in color NHJ 2250 French Pumpkin (D)
- 1 skein in color NHJ5185 Spring Green (E)

NEEDLES & NOTIONS

Size US 7 (4.5mm) 24" (61cm)-long circular knitting needle
Size US 6 (4mm) 24" (61cm)-long circular knitting needle
Stitch markers
Yarn needle
½yd (.5m) backing fabric
Matching sewing thread and needle

GAUGE

20 sts and 22 rows = 4" (10cm) in Stockinette st with smaller needle

Notes

Pillow front piece is worked back and forth in rows on circular needle. Border is worked in the round on stitches picked up around edges of front piece. Carry color not in use loosely along WS of work. Pick up new color from under old color to twist yarns and prevent holes.

Front Panel

With smaller needle and A, cast on 73 sts. Work in St st until piece measures 3" (8cm) from beginning. Change to B and knit 2 rows, purl 1 row for reverse ridge.

Begin Chart

Change to larger circular needle.
Row 1 (RS): K1 for selvedge st; beginning and ending where indicated, work Chart (page 67) across 71 sts, k1 for selvedge st. Keeping selvedge sts in St st, repeat 16 rows of chart until piece measures 10" (25cm) from beginning.
Change to smaller needle and B, purl 1 row, knit 2 rows for ridge.
Change to A and work in St st for 3" (8cm) more.
Bind off.

Mitered Border

With RS facing, smaller needle and B, pick up and knit 71 sts across cast-on edge of front panel, place marker, pick up and knit 1 st in corner, pick up and knit 65 sts along side edge, pick up and knit 1 st in corner, pick up and knit 71 sts across bound-off edge, place marker, pick up and knit 1 st in corner, pick up and knit 65 sts along opposite side edge, pick up and knit 1 st in corner—276 sts. Join to work in rounds; place marker for beginning of round.

Mitered Ridge

Rnd 1: Purl to marker, k1 for corner st; repeat around.
Increase Rnd: *Purl to marked corner st, M1, k1 for corner st, M1; repeat from *.
Rnd 3: Knit.
Change to C and repeat 3 rounds of Mitered Ridge.
Change to A and repeat 3 rounds of Mitered Ridge.
Change to E and repeat 3 rounds of Mitered Ridge.
Bind off.

Finishing

Work 5 lazy daisy stitches (see page 41) with C evenly spaced in A sections. Work a French knot (see page 41) with B in the center of each embroidered flower. Work small cross in the center of each motif with straight stitches and a contrasting color. Work a small diagonal stitch across the intersection of each cross. Weave in ends.

Making Pillow

Block the pillow top to a 16" (41cm) square.
Cut a 17" (43cm) square from backing fabric.
With RS together and using a ½" (1cm) seam allowance, sew pillow front to backing fabric along three sides.
Turn Right Side out.
Insert pillow form.
Whipstitch last side closed.

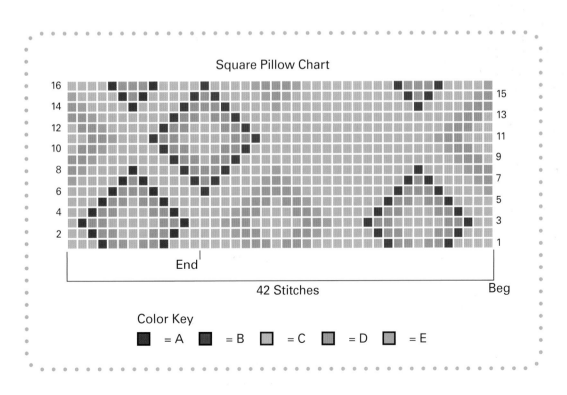

Square Pillow Chart

42 Stitches

End

Beg

Color Key
■ = A   ■ = B   ■ = C   ■ = D   ■ = E

T-Shirt Rug

This creative rug made from recycled T-shirts is perfect for brightening up a bathroom or kitchen. Worked in a basic Garter stitch on big needles, it's a great beginner project and is eco-friendly, too.

Design by **Candi Jensen**
Finished Measurements: **24" × 36"**
(61cm × 91cm)
Difficulty: **Easy**

Materials List

YARN

Cotton T-shirts (old or new) in size X-large or larger

- 5 white
- 4 medium blue
- 4 turquoise
- 3 green

1 skein white cotton yarn

NEEDLES & NOTIONS

Size US 17 (12.75mm) needles

Large eye yarn needle

GAUGE

4 sts = 4" (10cm) in Garter st

With color of your choice cast on 12 sts and work in Garter st, changing to other colors by knotting the T-shirts together. It is best to be random in your color changes and make some stripes wide and some narrow. Work until piece is approx 24" (61cm) long.

Finishing

Sew strips together with the white cotton yarn and a large eye yarn needle.

Making the Yarn

Pre-wash and dry the t-shirts. Cut off the top of each T-shirt, just at the armholes. Cut each shirt into one long strip, 1" (3cm) wide. Roll each one into a ball.

Knitting the Rug (make 3)

The rug is made in 3 12" (30cm)-wide strips.

Cable Knit Throw

Wrap yourself up in this charming afghan with its simple repeat of a Cable and Lace pattern. Once you get the hang of this pattern, you'll want to make one for every room.

*Design by **Brenda Lewis***
*Finished Measurements: **43" × 58"***
(109cm × 147cm)
*Difficulty: **Intermediate***

Materials List

YARN
5 skeins Red Heart Super Saver (100% acrylic) in color 631 Light Sage

NEEDLES & NOTIONS
Size US 10 (6mm) 36" (91cm)-long Circular Knitting Needle

Cable needle

2 stitch markers

Yarn needle

GAUGE
18 sts and 25 rows = 5" (13cm) in pattern.

Bottom Border

Cast on 155 sts. Do not join but work back and forth in rows.

Row 1 (RS): K1, * p1, k1; rep from * across.

Rows 2–5: Rep Row 1.

Row 6: K1, [p1, k1] twice, place marker on needle, work to last 5 sts; place marker on needle, k1, [p1, k1] twice.

Cable Pattern

Continue to work first and last 5 sts of every row in Border pattern and beg working Cable pattern on sts between markers as follows:

Row 1: *K4, yo, SSK, p7, k2tog, yo, k3; rep from * to last st; k1.

Row 2: *P6, k7, p5; rep from * to last st; p1.

Row 3: *K3, [yo, SSK] twice, p5, [k2tog, yo] twice, k2; rep from * to last st, k1.

Row 4: *P7, k5, p6; rep from * to last st; p1.

Row 5: *K2, [yo, SSK] three times, p3, [k2tog, yo] three times, k1; rep from * to last st; k1.

Row 6: *P8, k3, p7; rep from * to last st; p1.

Row 7: K1, *[yo, SSK] four times, k1, [k2tog, yo] four times, k1; rep from * across.

Row 8: *K2, p15, k1; rep from * to last st; k1.

Row 9: *P2, [yo, SSK] three times, k3, [k2tog, yo] three times, p1; rep from * to last st; p1.

Row 10: *K3, p13, k2; rep from * to last st; k1.

Row 11: *P3, [yo, SSK] twice, k5, [k2tog, yo] twice, p2; rep from * to last st; p1.

Row 12: *K4, p11, k3; rep from * to last st; k1.

Row 13: *P4, yo SSK, k7, k2tog, yo, p3; rep from * to last st; p1.

Row 14: *K5, p9, k4; rep from * to last st; k1.

Row 15: *P5, k9, p4; rep from * to last st; p1.

Rows 16 and 18: Rep Row 14.

Row 17: Rep Row 15.

Cable Knit Throw

Row 19: *P5; slip next 5 sts onto cable needle and hold at back of work, k4, then k5 from cable needle—cable made; p4; rep from * to last st; p1.

Rows 20, 22, and 24: Rep Row 14.

Rows 21 and 23: Rep Row 15.

Row 25: *P4, k2tog, yo, k7, yo, SSK, p3; rep from * to last st; p1.

Row 26: *K4, p11, k3; rep from * to last st; k1.

Row 27: *P3, [k2tog, yo] twice, k5, [yo, SSK] twice, p2; rep from * to last st; p1.

Row 28: *K3, p13, k2; rep from * to last st; k1.

Row 29: *P2, [k2tog, yo] three times, k3, [yo, SSK] three times, p1; rep from * to last st; p1.

Row 30: * K2, P15, K1; rep from * to last st; K1.

Row 31: K1, * [K2tog, yo] four times, K1, [yo, SSK] four times, K1; rep from * across.

Row 32: * P8, K3, P7; rep from * to last st; P1.

Row 33: * K2, [K2tog, yo] three times, P3, [yo, SSK] three times, K1; rep from * to last st; K1.

Row 34: * P7, K5, P6; rep from * to last st; P1.

Row 35: * K3, [K2tog, yo] twice, P5, [yo, SSK] twice, K2; rep from * to last st; K1.

Row 36: * P6, K7, P5; rep from * to last st; P1.

Row 37: * K4, K2tog, yo, P7, yo, SSK, K3; rep from * to last st; K1.

Row 38: * P5, K9, P4; rep from * to last st; P1.

Row 39: * K5, P9, K4; rep from * to last st; K1.

Rows 40 and 42: Rep Row 38.

Row 41: Rep Row 39.

Row 43: K5, P9, * cable, P9; rep to last 5 sts; K5.

Rows 44, 46, and 48: Rep Row 38.

Rows 45 and 47: Rep Row 39.

Rep Rows 1–48 four more times, then rep Rows 1–38 once more. Remove stitch markers on last row.

Top Border

Work 6 rows same as for Bottom Border.

Bind off loosely in pattern.

Entrelac Pillow

Entrelac Pillow

The fascinating entrelac technique is wonderful for a variety of projects, and this pillow is a perfect introduction. It's worked in two complementary colors, and you won't have to worry about tricky shaping.

Design by **Jenn Jarvis**
Dimensions: **14" (36cm) × 14" (36cm)**
Difficulty: **Intermediate**

Materials List

YARN
Red Heart Soft Yarn (256 yds [230m])
- 1 skein in color 9114 Honey (A)
- 1 skein in color 9518 Teal (B)

NEEDLES & NOTIONS
Size US 7 (4.5mm) needles
Yarn needle
14" × 14" (36cm × 36cm) pillow form

GAUGE
16 sts and 21 rows = 4" (10cm) in Stockinette st.

Pillow Front
With A, cast on 42 sts.

Base Triangles
Row 1 (RS): K1, turn.
Row 2 and all WS Rows: Purl all sts in this section, turn.
Row 3: Sl 1, k1, turn.
Row 5: Sl 1, k2, turn.
Row 7: Sl 1, k3, turn.
Row 9: Sl 1, k4, turn.
Row 11: Sl 1, k5, do not turn.
Repeat Rows 1–11 six times more—7 Triangles.
Change to B.

First Rectangle Row
Left Edge Triangle
Row 1 (WS): K1, turn.
Row 2: K in front and back loops, turn.
Row 3: K1, p2tog (one st B, one st A), turn.
Row 4: K1, M1, k1, turn.
Row 5: K1, p1, p2tog, turn.
Rows 6, 8, and 10: K to last st, M1, k1, turn.
Row 7: K1, P2, p2tog, turn.
Row 9: K1, P3, p2tog, turn.
Row 11: K1, P4, p2tog. Do not turn.

Rectangles Row 1 (WS): With Wrong Side facing, pick up and p6 sts along edge of next Triangle. Sl last st picked up onto left needle and p2tog (one st B, one st A), turn.
Rows 2, 4, 6, 8, and 10: K6, turn.
Rows 3, 5, 7, and 9: Sl 1, p4, p2tog, turn.
Row 11: Sl 1, P4, p2tog. Do not turn.
Repeat Rows 1–11 five times more across row.

Right Edge Triangle
Row 1 (WS): Pick up and p6 sts along edge of next Triangle, turn.
Row 2 and all RS Rows: Knit.
Row 3: Sl 1, P3, k2tog, turn.
Row 5: Sl 1, P2, k2tog, turn.
Row 7: Sl 1, P1, k2tog, turn.
Row 9: Sl 1, k2tog, turn.
Row 11: K2tog, turn and place remaining st on right-hand needle. Remaining st will be first st picked up for first Left Ege Rectangle. Change to A.

Second Rectangle Row

Row 1 (RS): With RS facing, pick up and k6 sts along edge of next Triangle or Rectangle. Sl last st picked up onto the left needle and SSK (one st A, one st B), turn.

Rows 2, 4, 6, 8, and 10: P6, turn.

Rows 3, 5, 7, and 9: Sl 1, k4, SSK, turn.

Row 11: Sl 1, K4, SSK. Do not turn.

Repeat Rows 1–11 six times more across row.

3rd Rectangle Row

Work same as First Rectangle Row except work across Rectangles.

Repeat Second and Third Rectangle Rows five times more.

Bind Off

Row 1 (RS): With RS facing, pick up and k6 sts along edge of next Triangle or Rectangle.

Row 2 and all WS Rows: Purl, turn.

Row 3: K2tog, k3, SSK, turn.

Row 5: K2tog, k2, SSK, turn.

Row 7: K2tog, k1, SSK, turn.

Row 9: K2tog, SSK, turn.

Row 11: Sl 1, SSK, psso. Do not turn. Remaining st will count as the first st of the next Triangle. Repeat Rows 1–11 six times more across row. Fasten off last st.

Pillow Back

With B, cast on 56 sts. Work in St st until piece measures 14" (36cm). Bind off.

Finishing

Sew Front to Back around 14" × 14" (36cm × 36cm) pillow form.

Afghan Square of the Week

Made from twelve different stitch patterns, this afghan is the perfect project for honing your knitting skills. You can start off easy then progress to the more difficult stitches, all the while making yourself a beautiful afghan.

*Finished Measurements: **30" × 40"** (76cm × 102cm)*
*Difficulty: **Intermediate***

Materials List

YARN

Red Heart Super Saver (100% acrylic, 364yd [328m])

- 1 skein in color 0885 Delft Blue (A)
- 1 skein in color 0381 Light Blue (B)
- 1 skein in color 0382 Country Blue (C)
- 1 skein in color 0886 Blue (D)

NEEDLES & NOTIONS

Size US 8 (5mm) needles

Size US 1/9 (5.5mm) crochet hook

Cable needle

Yarn needle

GAUGE

Finished square = 10" (25cm)

Notes

Pattern Stitches

3-st RPC: Slip 1 st to cable needle and hold in back, k2, p1 from cable needle.

3-st lPC: Slip 2 sts to cable needle and hold in front, p1, k2 from cable needle.

4-st lC: Slip 2 sts to cable needle and hold to front, k2, k2 from cable needle.

4-st RC: Slip 2 sts to cable needle and hold in back, k2, k2 from cable needle.

5-st lC: Slip 2 sts to cable needle and hold in front, k3, k2 from cable needle.

5-st PlC: Slip 2 sts to cable needle and hold in front, p1, k2, k2 from cable needle.

5-st lPC: Slip 2 sts to cable needle and hold in front, k2; p1, k2 from cable needle.

Cluster st: Wyif slip 5, dropping extra 2 wraps of each st, [bring yarn to back between needles, slip 5 sts back to left-hand needle, bring yarn to front between needles, slip 5 sts to right-hand needle] twice.

IT: Skip first st, passing behind skipped st, knit 2nd st-tbl, knit skipped st through front loop, drop both sts from left-hand needle.

MB (Make Bobble): Knit into front, back, front, back and front of st—5 sts made, turn; p5, turn; k2tog, k1, k2tog, turn; slip 1, p2tog, pass slip st over, slip st to right-hand needle.

RT: K2tog, leave sts on left-hand needle, insert right-hand needle from front between the 2 sts just knit together and knit the first st again. Slip both sts to right-hand needle together.

Square 1—Simple Basketweave

(Multiple of 8 sts)

With C, cast on 40 sts.

Row 1 (RS): Knit.

Rows 2–6: *K4, p4; repeat from * to end.

Row 7: Knit.

Rows 8–12: *P4, k4; repeat from * to end.

Repeat Rows 1–12 until piece

measures 10" (25cm) from beginning.

Bind off.

Square 2—Turnpike

(Multiple of 4 sts, excluding borders)

With A, cast on 38 sts.

Border Rows: With A, knit two rows.

Rows 1, 3, 5 and 7 (RS): With A, knit.

Rows 2, 4, 6 and 8: With A, k3, purl to last 3 sts, k3.

Row 9: K3 with A, k1 with B, *sl2wyib, sl2wyif; repeat from * to last 6 sts, sl2wyib, k1 with B, join second ball of A and k3.

Row 10: K3 with A, p1 with B, sl2wyif, *sl2wyib, sl2wyif; repeat from * to last 4 sts, p1 with B, k3 with A.

Rows 11 and 13: With A, knit.

Rows 12 and 14: With A, k3, purl to last 3 sts, k3.

Row 15: K3 with A, k1 with B, *sl2wyib, sl2wyif; repeat from * to last 6 sts, sl2wyib, k1 with B, k3 with A.

Row 16: K3 with A, p1 with B, sl2wyif, *sl2wyib, sl2wyif; repeat from * to last 4 sts, p1 with B, k3 with A.

Rows 17, 19, 21 and 23: With A, knit.

Rows 18, 20, 22 and 24: With A, k3, purl to last 3 sts, k3.

Row 25: K3 with A, k1 with D, *sl2wyib, sl2wyif; repeat from * to last 6 sts, sl2wyib, k1 with D, k3 with A.

Row 26: K3 with A, p1 with D, sl2wyif, *sl2wyib, sl2wyif; repeat from * to last 4 sts, p1 with D, k3 with A.

Rows 27 and 29: With A, knit.

Rows 28 and 30: With A, k3, purl to last 3 sts, k3.

Row 31: K3 with A, k1 with D, *sl2wyib, sl2wyif; repeat from * to last 6 sts, sl2wyib, k1 with D, k3 with A.

Row 32: K3 with A, p1 with B, sl2wyif, *sl2wyib, sl2wyif; repeat from * to last 4 sts, p1 with D, k3 with A.

Repeat Rows 1–32 until piece measures 9½" (24cm) from beginning.

Border Rows: With A, knit two rows.

Bind off.

Square 3—Seed Stitch Blocks

(Multiple of 7 sts + 5)

With C, cast on 40 sts.

Rows 1, 3 and 5 (RS): *[K1, p1] twice, k1, k2; repeat
from *, end [k1, p1] twice, k1.

Rows 2, 4 and 6: *[K1, p1] twice, k1, p2; repeat from *,
end [k1, p1] twice, k1.

Row 7: Purl.

Row 8: Knit.

Repeat Rows 1–8 until piece measures 10" (25cm)
from beginning.

Bind off.

Square 4—Daisy Chain

(Multiple of 6 sts + 1)

With B, cast on 43 sts.

Row 1 (RS): With B, knit.

Row 2: With B, knit.

Row 3: With B, k1, *[k1 wrapping yarn around
needle three times] five times, k1; repeat from * to end.

Row 4: With B, *k1, cluster st; repeat from * to last st, k1.

Rows 5 and 6: With B, knit.

Rows 7 and 9: With C, knit.

Rows 8 and 10: With C, purl.

Rows 11 and 12: With B, knit.

Row 13: With B, k4, *[k1 wrapping yarn around needle
three times] five times, k1; repeat from * to last 3 sts, k3.

Row 14: With B, k3, *k1, cluster st; repeat from * to last
4 sts, k4.

Rows 15 and 16: With B, knit.

Rows 17 and 19: With C, knit.

Rows 18 and 20: With C, purl.

Repeat Rows 1–20 until piece measures 10" (25cm)
from beginning.

Bind off.

Square 5—Jubilee Diamond

Pattern is established by working a Side Panel,
Diamond Panel and a Side Panel.

With B, cast on 51 sts.

Row 1: K1, work 15 sts of Side Panel, 19 sts of Diamond
Panel, 15 sts of Side Panel, k1. Work in patterns as
established, keeping first and last st in Garter st, until
piece measures 10" (25cm) from beginning. Bind off.

Side Panel

(Multiple of 15 sts)

Row 1 (RS): LT, p1, 4-st RC, p1, 4-st RC, p1, LT.
Row 2: P2, k1, p4, k1, p4, k1, p2.
Row 3: LT, p1, k4, p1, k4, p1, LT.
Row 4: P2, k1, p4, k1, p4, k1, p2.
Repeat Rows 1–4 for Side Panel.

Diamond Panel

(Multiple of 19 sts)

Row 1 (RS): P7, 5-st LC, p7.
Row 2: K7, p2, k1, p2, k7.
Row 3: P6, 3-st RPC, k1, 3-st LPC, p6.
Row 4: K6, p3, k1, p3, k6.
Row 5: P5, 3-st RPC, p1, k1, p1, 3-st LPC, p5.
Row 6: K5, p2, [k1, p1] twice, k1, p2, k5.
Row 7: P4, 3-st RPC, [k1, p1] twice, k1, 3-st LPC, p4.
Row 8: K4, p2, [p1, k1] three times, p3, k4.
Row 9: P3, 3-st RPC, [p1, k1] three times, p1, 3-st LPC, p3.
Row 10: K3, p2, [k1, p1] four times, k1, p2, k3.
Row 11: P2, 3-st RPC, [k1, p1] twice, MB, [p1, k1] twice, 3-st LPC, p2.
Row 12: K2, p2, [p1, k1] five times, p3, k2.
Row 13: P2, 3-st LPC, [k1, p1] four times, k1, 3-st RPC, p2.
Row 14: K3, p2, [k1, p1] four times, k1, p2, k3.
Row 15: P3, 3-st LPC, [p1, k1] three times, p1, 3-st RPC, p3.
Row 16: K4, p2, [p1, k1] three times, p3, k4.
Row 17: P4, 3-st LPC, [k1, p1] twice, k1, 3-st RPC, p4.
Row 18: K5, p2, [k1, p1] twice, k1, p2, k5.
Row 19: P5, 3-st LPC, p1, k1, p1, 3-st RPC, p5.
Row 20: K6, p3, k1, p3, k6.
Row 21: P6, 3-st LPC, k1, 3-st RPC, p6.

Row 22: K7, p2, k1, p2, k7.
Row 23: P7, 5-st PLC, p7.
Row 24: K7, p5, k7.
Row 25: P7, 5-st LPC, p7.
Row 26: K7, p2, k1, p2, k7.
Repeat Rows 3–26 for Diamond Panel.

Square 6—Wrap Mock Cable

(Multiple of 4 sts)
With D, cast on 56 sts.
Preparation Row (WS): *P3, k1; repeat from * to end.
Row 1 (RS): *P1, sl1, k2, psso k2; repeat from * to end.
Row 2: *P1, yo, p1, k1; repeat from * to end.
Row 3: *P1, k3; repeat from * to end.
Row 4: *P3, k1; repeat from * to end.
Row 5: *P1, sl1, k2, psso k2; repeat from * to end.
Row 6: *P1, yo, p1, k1; repeat from * to end.
Repeat Rows 1–6 until piece measures 10" (25cm) from beginning.
Bind off.

Square 7—Acorns

(Multiple of 8 sts)

With A, cast on 48 sts.

Rows 1 and 7 (WS): *P1, k2, p2, k2, p1;
repeat from *to end.

Row 2: *K1, p1, RT, LT, p1, k1; repeat from * to end.

Row 3: *P1, k1, p1, k2, p1, k1, p1; repeat from * to end.

Row 4: *K1, RT, p2, LT, k1; repeat from * to end.

Row 5: *P2, k4, p2; repeat from * to end.

Row 6: Knit.

Row 8: *LT, p1, k2, p1, RT; repeat from * to end.

Row 9: *K1, p1, k1, p2, k1, p1, k1; repeat from * to end.

Row 10: *P1, LT, k2, RT, p1; repeat from * to end.

Row 11: *K2, p4, k2; repeat from * to end.

Row 12: Knit.

Repeat Rows 1–12 until piece measures 10" (25cm)
from beginning.

Bind off.

Square 8—Bells & Rib

(Multiple of 5 sts + 1, excluding border)

With D, cast on 40 sts.

Rows 1 and 2: Knit.

Row 3 (RS): K2, k1, *p4, k1; repeat from * to last 2 sts, k2.

Row 4: K2, p1, *k4, p1; repeat from * to last 2 sts, k2.

Rows 5 and 6: Repeat Rows 3 and 4.

Row 7: K2, k1, *p2, cast on 4 sts, p2, k1; repeat from *
to last 2 sts, k2.

Row 8: K2, p1, *k2, purl into front and back of each of 4
cast-on sts, k2, p1; repeat from * to last 2 sts, k2.

Row 9: K2, k1, *p2, SKP, k4, k2tog, p2, k1; repeat from *
to last 2 sts, k2.

Row 10: K2, p1, *k2, p6, k2, p1; repeat from *
to last 2 sts, k2.

Row 11: K2, k1, *p2, SKP, k2, k2tog, p2, k1; repeat from *
to last 2 sts, k2.

Row 12: K2, p1, *k2, p4, k2, p1; repeat from * to last 2
sts, k2.

Row 13: K2, k1, *p2, SKP, k2tog, p2, k1; repeat from * to
last 2 sts, k2.

Row 14: K2, p1,*k1, p2tog, p2tog-tbl, k1, p1; repeat from *
to last 2 sts, k2.

Repeat Rows 3–12 until piece measures 9¹/₂" (24cm)
from beginning.

Knit 2 rows.

Bind off.

Square 9—Pueblo

(Multiple of 8 sts)

With D, cast on 40 sts.

Row 1 (RS): With D, *k4, wyib sl1, k3; repeat from * to end.

Row 2: With D, *p3, sl1wyif, p4; repeat from * to end.

Row 3: With B, *k2, [k1, wyib sl1] three times; repeat from * to end.

Row 4: With B, *[sl1wyif, p1] three times, p2; repeat from * to end.

Row 5: With D, *[wyib sl1, k1] three times, k2; repeat from * to end.

Row 6: With D, *p2, [p1, sl1wyif] three times; repeat from * to end.

Row 7: With B, *k3, wyib sl1, k4; repeat from * to end.

Row 8: With B, *p4, sl1wyif, p3; repeat from * to end.

Row 9: With D, * wyib sl1, k7; repeat from * to end.

Row 10: With D, *p7, sl1wyif; repeat from * to end.

Row 11: With B, *[k1, wyib sl1] twice, k3, wyib sl1; repeat from * to end.

Row 12: With B, *sl1wyif, p3, [sl1wyif, p1] twice; repeat from * to end.

Row 13: With D, *wyib sl1, k3, [wyib sl1, k1] twice; repeat from * to end.

Row 14: With D, *[p1, sl1wyif] twice, p3, sl1wyif; repeat from * to end.

Row 15: With B, *k7, wyib sl1; repeat from * to end.

Row 16: With B, *sl1wyif, p7; repeat from * to end.

Repeat Rows 1–16 until piece measures 10" (25cm) from beginning.

Bind off.

Square 10—Mini Diamond

(Multiple of 8 sts + 2)

With D, cast on 42 sts.

Row 1 (RS): K1, *k1, k2tog, yo, k1, yo, SSK, k2; repeat from * to last st, k1.

Row 2 and all WS rows: Purl.

Row 3: K1, *k2tog, yo, k3, yo, SSK, k1; repeat from * to last st, k1.

Row 5: K1, *yo, k5, yo, sl1, k2tog, psso; repeat from * to last st, k1.

Row 7: K1, *yo, SSK, k3, k2tog, yo, k1; repeat from * to last st, k1.

Row 9: K1, *k1, yo, SSK, k1, k2tog, yo, k2; repeat from * to last st, k1.

Row 11: K1, *k2, yo, sl1, k2tog, psso, yo, k3; repeat from * to last st, k1.

Row 12: Purl.

Repeat Rows 1–12 until piece measures 10" (25cm) from beginning.

Bind off.

Square 11—Tumbleweeds

(Multiple of 2 sts + 1)

With B, cast on 41 sts.

Row 1 (RS): K1 with B, *sl1wyif, k1 with B; repeat from * to end.

Row 2: With B, purl.

Row 3: K1 with A, *k1 with A, sl1wyif; repeat from * to last 2 sts, k2 with A.

Row 4: With A, purl.

Row 5: With A, knit.

Row 6: With A, purl.

Repeat Rows 1–6 until piece measures 10" (25cm) from beginning.

Bind off.

Square 12—Windswept

(Multiple of 5 sts + 1)

With B, cast on 56 sts.

Row 1 (RS): *P1, k4; repeat from * to last st, p1.

Row 2: K1, *p4, k1; repeat from * to end.

Row 3: *P1, 4-st LC; repeat from * to last st, p1.

Row 4: Repeat Row 2.

Repeat Rows 1–4 until piece measures 10" (25cm) from beginning.

Bind off.

Finishing

Because of the variety of stitches and patterns, squares may differ slightly in size from each other. Blocking them all to the same size before sewing them together will make assembly easier. Arrange squares in 3 × 4 pattern as desired. With RS together, whipstitch squares together into four rows of three squares each. Whipstitch rows together in like manner.

Border

Border is crocheted in rounds, all on the RS.

Rnd 1: With crochet hook, join D with sl st in upper right corner of afghan, ch 1, 3 sc in corner, work sc evenly spaced around edge of afghan, working 3 sc in each corner; join with sl st in first sc.

Rnd 2: Ch 2, work backwards and crochet around edge of afghan; join with sl st in first st.

Fasten off.

Weave in ends.

Wearables

In this chapter we share with you a few designs for you to wear. Our snuggly slippers are so easy to make you'll want to stitch them up in a variety of colors to match your every mood. The beautiful cable wrap sweater knits up with a wonderful drape and is perfect for every size. No matter what you are in the mood to wear, our designs are perfect for you.

Episode 308

Norah Gaughan Sweater

It's a wrap! Or is it a sweater? Somewhere in between it's sure to delight and be a very timely addition to any wardrobe. The body is made in a long rectangle using a Cable and Lace technique that gives this creative creation its beautiful drape.

Materials List

YARN
13 skeins Berroco Inca Gold (80% merino, 20% silk, 122 yds) in color 6424 Turquesa

NEEDLES & NOTIONS
Size US 7 (4.5mm) needles
Cable needle (cn)
2 stitch holders

GAUGE
20 sts and 28 rows = 4" (10cm) in Stockinette st
23 sts and 32 rows = 4" (10cm) in Cable Pattern

Notes
Body of this garment is knit in one piece from left front edge to right front edge.

Cable Pattern
(Multiple of 17 sts + 12)
Row 1 (RS): * K2tog, yo, k8, k2tog, yo, p2, k1, p2, rep from * to last 12 sts, end k2tog, yo, k8, k2tog, yo.

Design by **Norah Gaughan**
Finished Measurements: *46 (48, 51)" [117 (123, 130)cm] wide × 24 (24, 25)" [61 (61, 64)cm] long; body is knit from side to side, so the length is actually the width of piece. Shown in size Medium/Large. Directions are for Woman's size X-Small/Small. Changes for sizes Medium/Large and 1X/2X are in parentheses.*
Skill level: **Intermediate**

Row 2 and all WS rows: * P12, k5, rep from * to last 12 sts, end p12.
Row 3: * K2tog, yo, sl 4 sts to cn and hold in back, k4, k4 from cn, k2tog, yo, p2, k1, p2, rep from * to last 12 sts, end k2tog, yo, sl 4 sts to cn and hold in back, k4, k4 from cn, k2tog, yo.
Rows 5 and 7: Rep Row 1.
Row 8: Rep Row 1.
Rep Rows 1–8 for Cable Pattern.

Body
Cast on 137 (137, 143) sts.
Row 1 (RS): K2, p1 (1, 4), work Row 1 of Cable Pattern to last 3 (3, 6) sts, end p1 (1, 4), k2.
Row 2: K3 (3, 6), work Row 2 of Cable Pattern to last 3 (3, 6) sts, k to end. Work even in pattern as established until piece measures 10½" (27cm) from beg, end on WS.

Shape Left Armhole

Next Row (RS): Work 76 (76, 82) sts, then sl remaining 61 sts onto stitch holder for lower section.

Upper Section

Work 1 row even.

Dec Row 1 (RS): Work to last 2 sts, k2tog. Rep this dec every RS row twenty (twenty-four, twenty-six) times more—55 (51, 55) sts. Work even until Armhole measures 6 (6$\frac{1}{4}$, 6$\frac{1}{2}$)" [15 (16, 17)cm], end on WS. Sl sts onto second holder.

Lower Section

With RS facing, sl 61 sts from first holder onto straight needle. Join yarn and bind off 6 sts, work to end—55 sts. Work even for 1" (3cm), end on WS.

Inc Row (RS): K1, M1, work to end. Continue to inc at beg of every RS row in this manner, working incs into Cable Pattern as sts become available, twenty (twenty-four, twenty-six) times more, end on RS—76 (80, 82) sts. Joining Row (WS): Work 76 (80, 82) sts, cast on 6 sts, then work 55 (51, 55) sts from first holder—137 (137, 143) sts. Work even in Cable Pattern until piece measures 13 (14, 15)" [33 (36, 38)cm] above Joining Row, end on WS.

Shape Right Armhole

Next Row (RS): Work 55 (51, 55) sts, then sl remaining 82 (86, 88) sts onto first holder for Lower Section.

Upper Section

Work even for 1" (3cm), end on WS.

Inc Row (RS): Work to last st, M1, k1—56 (52, 56) sts. Continue to inc at end of every RS row in this manner twenty (twenty-four, twenty-six) times more, working incs into Cable Pattern as sts become available, end on RS—76 (76, 82) sts. Sl sts onto second holder.

Lower Section

With RS facing, sl 82 (86, 88) sts from first holder onto straight needle. Join yarn and bind off 6 sts, work to end—76 (80, 82) sts. Work 1 row even.

Dec Row (RS): K1, k2tog, work to end—75 (79, 81) sts. Continue to dec 1 st at beg of every RS row twenty (twenty-four, twenty-six) times more—55 sts. Work even for 1" (3cm), end on RS.

Joining Row (WS): Work 55 sts, cast on 6 sts, work 76 (76, 82) sts from second holder—137 (137, 143) sts. Work even in Cable Pattern until piece measures 10$\frac{1}{2}$ (11, 11$\frac{1}{2}$)" [27 (28, 29)cm] above Joining Row, end on WS. Bind off.

Sleeves

With straight needles, cast on 45 sts. Work even in St st for 1" (3cm), end on WS.

Inc Row (RS): K2, M1, k to last 2 sts, M1, k2—47 sts. Rep this inc every 2 (1, $\frac{3}{4}$)" [5 (3, 2)cm] four (seven, nine) times more—55 (61, 65) sts. Work even until sleeve measures 9" (23cm) from beg, end on WS.

Shape Cap

Dec Row (RS): K2, k2tog, k to last 4 sts, SSK, k2—53 (59, 63) sts. Rep this dec every RS row twenty-two times more, end on WS—9 (15, 19) sts. Bind off 2 sts at beg of the next 2 rows.
Bind off remaining 5 (11, 15) sts.

Finishing

Sew Sleeve seams. Sew Sleeve Caps into Armholes with Sleeve seams at points marked with X on schematic (page 89).

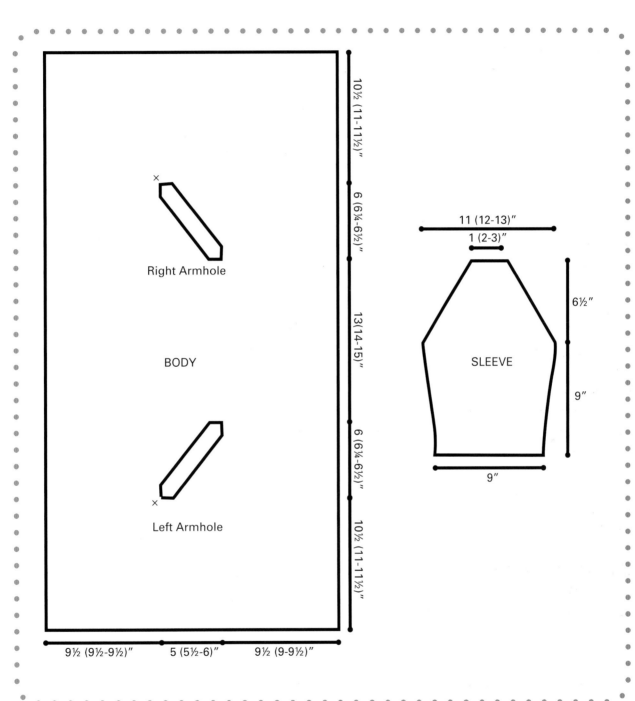

Right Armhole

BODY

Left Armhole

10½ (11-11½)"

6 (6¼-6½)"

13(14-15)"

6 (6¼-6½)"

10½ (11-11½)"

9½ (9½-9½)"   5 (5½-6)"   9½ (9-9½)"

11 (12-13)"

1 (2-3)"

SLEEVE

6½"

9"

9"

Slipper Socks

Put a little pep in your step with these quick to stitch slippers. Made with simple shaping and in worsted weight yarn you can work them up in a rainbow of colors and they make a great gift.

Materials List

YARN

1 skein Caron Simply Soft (100% Acrylic, 315yd [284m]) in color 9705 Sage

NEEDLES & NOTIONS

Size US 7 (4.5mm) needles

1 pair Boye slipper sock bottoms

No. 22 tapestry needle

Stitch holder

Stitch markers

GAUGE

20 sts = 4" (10cm) in Stockinette st

*Design by **Kim Guzman***

*Finished Measurements: **Directions are given for size Small. Size Medium and Large are in parentheses.***

Small (9" [23cm])

fits Women's US shoesizes 6-7½

Medium (9½" [24cm])

fits Women's US shoe sizes 8-8½

Large (10" [25cm])

fits Women's US shoe sizes 9-10

*Difficulty: **Intermediate***

Notes

Make two.

Sl first st on every row to make a firm edge.

Top

CO 46 (50, 50) sts loosely, leaving 20" (51cm) tail for sewing side seam.

Row 1: Sl1, [p1, k1] across, end with p1.

Rep Row 1 for 6" (15cm) or desired length.

Begin Heel

K across 20 (22, 22) sts. Place rem 26 (28, 28) sts on holder for Instep.

Work Heel Flap in St st (knit one row, purl one row) for 2¾ (3, 3)" [7 (8, 8)cm]; end with purl row. Bind off next row (knit row) tightly. (1 st rem on needle)

Gusset and Instep

With RS facing, put 9 (11, 11) sts along inside edge of Heel Flap (1 st is already on needle)—10 (12, 12) sts. K2 from holder, pm, work in rib pattern across 22 (24, 24) sts (from holder), pm, k last 2 sts from holder. Turn, CO 10 (12, 12) sts for opposite Gusset—46 (52, 52) sts.

Shape Gussets

Row 1 (WS): Sl1, p to marker, rib to next marker, p to end.

Row 2 (RS): Sl1, k to 2 sts before first marker, k2tog, rib to next marker, (sl1, k1, psso), knit to end—44 (50, 50) sts.

Rep Rows 1-2 five (seven, seven) times more—34 (36, 36) sts.

Rep Row 1 once more.

Work Instep

Row 1 (RS): Sl1 [p1, k1] two times, p1, slip marker, (sl1, k1, psso), k to last 2 sts before next marker, k2tog, [p1, k1] three times—32 (34, 34) sts.

Row 2 (WS): Rib to marker, p to next marker, rib to end.
Rep Rows 1–2 one (on, zero) times more—30 (32, 34) sts.

Foot

Row 1 (RS): Rib to marker, k to next marker, rib to end.

Row 2 (WS): Rib to marker, p to next marker, rib to end.
Rep Rows 1–2 until Sock measures 7 (7½, 8)" [18 (19, 20)cm] from beg of Gusset shaping, end with WS row.

Shape Toe

Row 1 (RS): Sl1, rib to marker, (sl1, k1, psso) two times, k to 4 sts before marker, k2tog twice, rib to end—26 (28, 30) sts.

Row 2 (WS): Sl1, rib to marker, p to next marker, rib to end.
Rep Rows 1–2 once more, remove markers after last row—22 (24, 26) sts.

Row 5: Sl1, rib 3 sts, (sl1, k1, psso) twice, k to last 8 sts, k2tog twice, rib to end—18 (20, 22) sts.

Row 6: Sl1, rib 3 sts, p to last 4 sts, rib to end.

Row 7: (Sl1, k1, psso) three times , k to last 6 sts, (k2tog) three times—12 (14, 16) sts.
Bind off all stitches in purl.

Finishing

With needle, seam Cuff, Heel and Gusset. Center Heel on back seam of Sole bottom with center of Toe to front of sole, fitted to the inside of the Sole sides. Pin evenly around (safety pins or split ring markers work well). With needle, whipstitch Slipper Top to Sole.

Leaf-Lace Tank Top

Pretty in pink, this stylish tank has a Leaf-Lace inset that artfully splits and travels up the V-neck. It's worked partially in the round so you have no side seams to worry about.

Finished Measurements: *X-Small (Small, Medium, Large, X-Large, 2X). Finished Bust 35 (37, 39, 41, 43, 45) [89 (94, 99, 104, 109, 114)cm]. Directions are for size X-Small. Changes for sizes Small, Medium, Large, X-Large, 2X are in parentheses*
Difficulty: **Intermediate**

Leaf-Lace Tank Top

Notes

Top is knit in the Rnd from the bottom to Armholes. It is then divided into Front and Back and worked in rows.

Leaf-Lace Pattern

(Worked over 26 sts in the Rnd)

The number of stitches in the Leaf-Lace Pattern changes on each row, beginning and ending with 26 sts.

Rnd 1: P2, k7, k2tog, yo, k1, yo, p2, yo, k1, yo, SSK, k7, p2—28 sts.

Rnd 2: P2, k6, k2tog, k3, p2, k3, SSK, k6, p2—26 sts.

Rnd 3: P2, k5, k2tog, (k1, yo) two times, k1, p2, k1, (yo, k1) two times, SSK, k5, p2—28 sts.

Rnd 4: P2, k4, k2tog, k5, p2, k5, SSK, k4, p2—26 sts.

Rnd 5: P2, k3, k2tog, k2, yo, k1, yo, k2, p2, k2, yo, k1, yo, k2, SSK, k3, p2—28 sts.

Rnd 6: P2, k2, k2tog, k7, p2, k7, SSK, k2, p2—26 sts.

Rnd 7: P2, k1, k2tog, k3, yo, k1, yo, k3, p2, k3, yo, k1, yo, k3, SSK, k1, p2—28 sts.

Rnd 8: P2, k2tog, k9, p2, k9, SSK, p2—26 sts.

Repeat Rnds 1–8 for Leaf-Lace Pattern.

Left Leaf-Lace Pattern

(Worked over 13 sts in rows)

The number of stitches in Leaf-Lace Pattern changes on each row, beginning and ending with 13 sts.

Row 1: P2, k7, k2tog, yo, k1, yo, p1—14 sts.

Row 2: P4, p2tog, p6, k2—13 sts.

Row 3: P2, k5, k2tog, (k1, yo) two times, k1, p1—14 sts.

Row 4: P6, p2tog, p4, k2—13 sts.

Row 5: P2, k3, k2tog, k2, yo, k1, yo, k2, p1—14 sts.

Row 6: P8, p2tog, p2, k2—13 sts.

Row 7: P2, k1, k2tog, k3, yo, k1, yo, k3, p1—14 sts.

Row 8: P10, p2tog, k2—13 sts.

Repeat Rows 1–8 for Left Leaf-Lace Pattern.

Right Leaf-Lace Pattern

(Worked over 13 sts in rows)

The number of stitches in Leaf-Lace Pattern changes on each row, beginning and ending with 13 sts.

Row 1: P1, yo, k1, yo, SSK, k7, p2—14 sts.

Row 2: K2, p6, p2tog-tbl, p4—13 sts.

Row 3: P1, k1, (yo, k1) two times, SSK, k5, p2—14 sts.

Row 4: K2, p4, p2tog-tbl, p6—13 sts.

Row 5: P1, k2, yo, k1, yo, k2, SSK, k3, p2—14 sts.

Row 6: K2, p2, p2tog-tbl, p8—13 sts.

Row 7: P1, k3, yo, k1, yo, k3, SSK, k1, p2—14 sts.

Row 8: K2, p2tog-tbl, p10—13 sts.

Repeat Rows 1–8 for Right Leaf-Lace Pattern.

Body

Cast on 176 (184, 196, 204, 216, 224) sts. Join to work in Rnds, being careful not to twist sts. Place marker for beginning of Rnd and side seam and a second marker after 88 (92, 98, 102, 108, 112) sts for opposite side seam. Purl 1 Rnd, knit 1 Rnd.

Rnd 1: *K31 (33, 36, 38, 41, 43), beginning with Rnd 1, work Leaf-Lace Pattern on 26 sts, knit 31 (33, 36, 38, 41, 43) for Back; repeat from * for Front.

Continue to work as established, repeat Rnds 1–8 of Leaf-Lace Pattern until piece measures 2½ (2½, 3, 3, 3½, 3½)" [6 (6, 8, 8, 9, 9)cm].

Decrease Rnd 1: *K20, sk2p, work in pattern to 20 sts before side marker, sk2p, k20; repeat from * once—168 (176, 188, 196, 208, 216) sts.

Work in patterns as established for 17 rows.

Decrease Rnd 2: *K19, sk2p, work in pattern to 20 sts before side marker, sk2p, k19; repeat from * once—160 (168, 180, 188, 200, 208) sts.

Work in patterns as established for 23 rows.

Increase Rnd 1: *K20, M1R, k1, M1L, work in pattern to 20 sts before side marker, M1R, k1, M1L, k20; repeat from * once—168 (176, 188, 196, 208, 216) sts.

Increase Rnd 2: *K20, M1R, k1, M1L, work in pattern to 20 sts before side marker, M1R, k1, M1L, k20; repeat from * once—176 (184, 196, 204, 216, 224) sts.

Work in pattern until piece measures 14 (14, 14½, 14½, 15, 15)" [36 (36, 37, 37, 38, 38)cm] from beginning, ending with an even number round.

Shape Armholes and Neck

Left Back Shoulder

Next Row (RS): Bind off 4 (4, 5, 5, 6, 6) sts for Armhole, knit to 2 sts before Leaf-Lace Pattern, SSK for Neck edge, work corresponding odd number row of Left Leaf-Lace Pattern. Slip remaining sts to stitch holder for Right Shoulder and Front.

Purl 1 row, working corresponding even number row of Left Leaf-Lace Pattern of across first 13 sts.

Decrease Row: K2, k2tog, work to 2 sts before Left Leaf-Lace Pattern, SSK, work to end. Purl 1 row, working corresponding even number row of Left Leaf-Lace Pattern across first 13 sts. Repeat last 2 rows three (three, four, four, five, five) more times—32 (34, 34, 36, 36, 38) sts.

Neck Decrease Row: Work to 2 sts before Left Leaf-Lace Pattern, SSK, work to end. Purl 1 row, working

corresponding even number row of Left Leaf Lace Pattern across first 13 sts. Repeat last 2 rows until 13 sts remain. Work as established until Armhole measures 7½ (7½, 8, 8, 8½, 9)" [19 (19, 20, 20, 22, 23)cm]. Bind off.

Right Back Shoulder

Slip 44 (46, 49, 51, 54, 56) sts from stitch holder to needle for Right Shoulder.

Next Row (RS): Join yarn and work corresponding odd number row of Right Leaf Lace Pattern across 13 sts, k2tog, knit to last 6 (6, 7, 7, 8, 8) sts, SSK, k2.

Next Row: Bind off 4 (4, 5, 5, 6, 6) sts for Armhole, purl across, working corresponding even number row of Right Leaf-Lace Pattern of across last 13 sts.

Decrease Row: Work Right Leaf-Lace Pattern across 13 sts, k2tog, work to last 4 sts, SSK, k2. Purl 1 row, working corresponding even number row of Right Leaf-Lace Pattern of across last 13 sts. Repeat last 2 rows two (two, three, three, four, four) more times—32 (34, 34, 36, 36, 38) sts.

Neck Decrease Row: Work Right Leaf Lace Pattern across 13 sts, k2tog, work to end. Purl 1 row, working corresponding even number row of Right Leaf-Lace Pattern of across first 13 sts. Repeat last 2 rows until 13 sts remain. Work as established until Armhole measures 7½ (7½, 8, 8, 8½, 9)".
Bind off.
Repeat Left and Right Shoulder on remaining sts for Front.

Finishing

Sew Shoulder seams.

Armhole Edging

With RS facing and shorter circular needle, pick up and k80 (80, 84, 84, 86, 90) stitches evenly around Armhole. Join to work in Rnds, place a marker for beginning of Rnd. Purl 1 Rnd.
Bind off loosely knitwise.
Weave in ends.

Quick Gifts

Knit projects are always a welcome gift for
anyone, and we have pulled together a few of our favorites
from the show. Stitch up the cat toy for that special cat
lover or make a bracelet for a friend. No matter what you
make, these gifts are sure to please and will take you no
time at all to whip up.

Cherry Bracelet and Barrette

Too cute felted cherries adorn this fashionable bracelet and matching barrette. The little cherries are easy to knit and felt. Then, just add some beads for the bracelet or a ribbon for the barrette, and you're ready to go.

Design by **Maggie Pace**
Finished Measurements: **Each cherry is an approximate ³/₄" (2cm) sphere**
Difficulty: **Easy**

Materials List

YARN

1 skein Pick Up Sticks wool (100% wool, 65yd [59m]) in color Red (Each cherry takes about 2 ¹/₂ yd [2m] to make. You can also use any 100% wool in worsted weight that will felt.)

NEEDLES & NOTIONS

Size US 10 (6mm) needles

Yarn needle

FOR THE BRACELET:

Beading needle

Needle-nose pliers

Eight or nine ¹/₈" (3mm) diameter seed beads

Eight or nine ³/₈" (3mm) circumference glass beads

8mm clear stretchy beading elastic

Silver crimp tubes

FOR THE BARRETTE

Black cord elastic

Blank 2" (5cm) metal barrette with holes on either side

10" (25cm) of ³/₈" (10mm) grosgrain ribbon

GAUGE

16 sts and 20 rows = 4" (10cm) unfelted. It is not critical to obtain gauge for this project, as the final size is determined mostly by how long the pieces felt.

Cherry Bracelet and Barrette

Cherries

For the bracelet make eight or nine Cherries, depending on wrist circumference; for the barrette, make two for one barrette.

Cast on 12 sts. Leave an 18" (46cm) tail (this is important, measure the tail to make sure).

Row 1: Knit.

Row 2: Purl.

Row 3: K2tog to the end of row—6 sts.

Row 4: P2tog to the end of row—3 sts.

Row 5: K3tog—1 st on needle.

Fasten off last st. Thread yarn needle with yarn coming from last st.

Assemble

1. Sew sides together, sewing from the center and working your way to the outer cast-on edge.

2. Using the same threaded needle, pick up stitches along the cast-on edge. In a moment, you'll pull these stitches to gather the circle into a ball.

3. Stuff the 18" (46cm) cast-on tail into the center of the bobble.

4. Now pull the yarn to gather. The cone-shaped bobble has turned into a fat little ball.

Make sure you weave in the end very securely before cutting so that it doesn't come unraveled during felting. Now you are ready to felt.

Felting

Felt all the Cherries at the same time by adding them to a mesh laundry bag or a pillowcase. Felt the Cherries before adding the Stems. Set washer to hot, on a heavy duty cycle with low water. Add the mesh laundry bag

with the Cherries to the water. It will take a few minutes for the pieces to show signs of shrinkage. Once they do, we recommend that you check them often, at least every 1–2 minutes. Pull out the pieces when they reach the desired size and texture. None of the stitches should be visible and the pieces should be stiff to the touch. Rinse by hand in cold water and roll in a towel to absorb excess water.

Don't be alarmed if the Cherry bobbles look a little misshapen. They aren't done until you roll them in your palms, as you would shape cookie dough into a ball. Once shaped, leave to dry.

Finishing
For Cherry Barrette

1. To make the Cherry Stem, cut a 4" (10cm) length of the elastic cord. Tie a knot at the very end of it. Thread the unknotted end with a yarn needle.

2. Insert the needle in the center bottom of the Cherry and pull it through to the top. Remove the needle. Trim elastic to the appropriate size for a Stem. Repeat with the second Cherry.

3. Measure the grosgrain ribbon against the barrette, then double its length. Fold the ribbon on itself and with a sewing needle and matching thread, sew in place. The ribbon is now a continuous loop slightly longer than the barrette. Complete the bow shape by centering the loop's seam and pinching at the middle. Cut a small piece of ribbon to wrap the center pinch. Sew in place at the back. Center the top of the Cherry Stems at the back seam and stitch in place, using an overcast stitch (see page 45). Connect to the barrette by sewing the bow at the holes on either side of the barrette.

For the Bracelet

1. Thread a beading needle with sewing thread and one of the seed beads. Secure it to the center of the Cherry bobble. Repeat with all bobbles.

2. Thread the yarn needle with the clear stretch elastic cord. Send the needle through the side of the beaded bobble so the seed bead on the bobble will end up at the top. Thread the larger bead onto the elastic, then another bobble. Repeat until the bracelet is the desired circumference. You'll need the needle-nose pliers to make threading easier.

3. Finally, tie off the Bracelet by threading each end through the tube crimp, then squeezing the crimp flat with the needle-nose pliers.

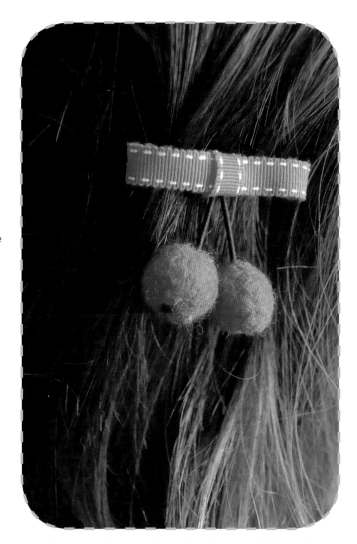

Catnip Toy

Your cat will enjoy hours of playtime with his new catnip friend. Worked in the round and then felted for extra strength, this toy will be able to stand up to even the toughest workout.

Design by **Maggie Pace**
Finished Measurements:
approx 3" (8cm) across
Difficulty: **Easy**

Cat Head

Using A, cast on 4 sts.

Row 1: Kfb into each st—8 sts.

Row 2: Pfb into each st—16 sts.

Row 3: Kfb into each st—32 sts.

Rows 4–10: Work in St st.

Rows 11–17: Change to B and work in St st.

Row 18: *P2tog. Repeat from * to end—16 sts.

Row 19: *K2tog. Repeat from * to end—8 sts.

Row 20: *P2tog. Repeat from * to end—4 sts.

Cut yarn and thread yarn needle with tail. Run tail back through sts and pull sts off needle. Pull to gather, like a purse string. Using the same needle, sew the side seams together, using an invisible seam for Stockinette stitch. At the end of the seam, leave a portion open to create a hole where the catnip can be inserted when the Toy is complete.

Ears (make 2)

Using A, cast on 6 sts.

Row 1: Knit.

Row 2: P2tog, p2, p2tog—4 sts.

Row 3: K2tog twice—2 sts.

Row 4: P2tog—1 st.

Cut yarn and fasten off last stitch. Weave in ends. Change to B and repeat Ears pattern. To finish the Ear, place the A and B pieces together, Wrong Sides touching each other and whipstitch together at all three edges using a yarn needle threaded with either A or B. Weave in ends. The stitches will disappear when the Ears are felted.

Arrange the Ears on the Cat Head as seen in the photo. Sew the Ears on the head at the color change line, ³/₄"–1" (2–3cm) apart.

Bobble Paws

Using A, cast on 12 sts, leaving a 12" (30cm) tail.

Row 1: Knit.

Row 2: Change to B and purl.

Row 3: *K2tog. Repeat from * to end—6 sts.

Row 4: *P2tog. Repeat from * to end—3 sts.

Row 5: K3tog—1 st.

Cut yarn and fasten off last stitch. Thread yarn needle with tail and sew together side seams using an invisible seam for Stockinette stitch. Stop at color change and weave in end. Rethread needle with A tail and finish the seam. At the end of the seam, use the yarn needle to pick up each stitch along the cast-on edge, then run the tail through all these stitches. Before gathering, stuff the cast-on tail into the center of the Bobble to give the Bobble more density.

Felting

Felt the Cat Head (with Ears already attached) and the four Paws separately. Place all pieces into a mesh laundry bag or a pillowcase tied off. Set the washer to the hottest, highest agitation cycle. Add the bag to the water and let it run through the cycle. Stop the machine before it goes into the spin cycle and check the work. The pieces are done when the Head measures 3", all pieces are stiff to the touch and their stitch definition has completely disappeared. Pull out and rinse in cool water. Lay flat and let air dry.

Finishing

Using yarn needle threaded with B, embroider the cat's face. All facial elements are created using a simple satin stitch.

For the Legs, hand crochet a chain 15 sts long, leaving 8" tails on each side. Repeat for second set of Legs. Thread the tail with a yarn needle and insert through the center of one of the Paws on the side that you want to be facing up. Return the needle through the Paw and back to the topside. Pass through the hand chain a few times to secure. Weave in end. Repeat with another Paw on the other side. Repeat this process, using the remaining two Paws and 15-stitch chain. Securely tack the chain at its midpoint on the underside of the Cat Head, at the color line. Repeat with the second chain. Add three satin stitches on each of the Paws to indicate Toes.

Add catnip through the hole (stretch hole open, if necessary), and sew closed. For a non-catnip Toy, stuff with polyester fiberfill.

Simple Satin Stitch

Bring the needle up through the fabric from back to front at one end of the stitch you'd like to place. Pierce needle back down through fabric at other end of stitch.

Kaffe Fassett Socks

Kaffe Fassett Socks

Get a leg up on great style with these colorful socks by Kaffe Fassett. The basic socks are easy to knit up, but it's the yarn that gives them the special look.

Design by **Kaffe Fassett**.
To Fit US Shoe Size: **Woman's 5 ¹/₂/6 (Woman's 7/7¹/₂, Woman's 8 ¹/₂/9, Woman's 10/Man's 9/10, Man's 11, Man's 12) [(36/37 (38/39, 40/41, 42/43, 44/45, 46/47)cm]**
Directions are for size **X-Small. Changes for sizes Small, Medium, Large, X-Large, XX-Large are in parentheses.**
Difficulty: **Intermediate**

Materials List

YARN
2 skeins Regia 4-Faedig Design Line Color (75% wool, 25% polyamide, 229yd [206m]), in color of your choice

NEEDLES & NOTIONS
Size US 2 (2.75mm) double-pointed needles (dpns)
Stitch holder
Stitch markers
Yarn needle

GAUGE
30 sts and 42 rows = 4" (10cm)

Notes
Make 2.

Short Rows
W&T = Bring yarn to front, slip next st, turn, wrap yarn around slipped st and slip same st back onto right-hand needle. On next row, work wrapped st by picking up wrap and working together with st on left-hand needle.

Body
Cast on 60 (60, 64, 64, 68, 72) sts. Divide sts evenly between dpns. Join to work in rounds, being careful not to twist sts. Place a marker for beginning of round.
Work in k1, p1 rib until piece measures 2" (5cm) from beginning.
Change to St st and knit until piece measures 9" (23cm) from beginning, ending 15 (15, 16, 16, 17, 18) sts before beginning marker.

Shape Heel
Knit across next 30 (30, 32, 32, 34, 36) sts for Heel. Slip remaining sts to a stitch holder for Foot.

Short Rows
Working on Heel sts only, purl to last st, W&T.
Knit to last st, W&T.
*Purl to 1 st before previous wrapped st, W&T.
Knit to 1 st before previous wrapped st, W&T.
Repeat from * until there are 5 (5, 7, 7, 7, 7) sts between wrapped sts, ending with a WS row.
Knit all stitches around including stitches on stitch holder for Foot.

Shape Foot
Knit 60 (60, 64, 64, 68, 72) sts until Foot measures 7 ¹/₄ (8, 8¹/₄, 8³/₄, 9, 9¹/₂)" [18 (20, 21, 22, 23, 24)cm], ending at beginning marker.

Shape Toe

Next Rnd: K15 (15, 16, 16, 17, 18) sts, place Toe marker, k30 (30, 32, 32, 34, 36) sts, place Toe marker, k15 (15, 16, 16, 17, 18) sts.

Decrease Rnd: [Work to 3 sts before next Toe marker, k2tog, k2, SSK] twice, knit to end of round.

Repeat Decrease Rnd every 4th row once, every 3rd round twice, every other round three (three, three, three, four, four) times, then every round six (six, seven, seven, seven, eight) times.

Divide remaining sts on two needles and graft stitches together.

Finishing

Weave in ends.

Knitting Basics

Here you'll find all of the basic hows-tos of knitting that you'll need to make the projects from the first three seasons of *Knit and Crochet Now!* in the preceding pages. Learn to do everything from casting on, to working basic stitches and binding off. You'll also find information on knitting needles and yarns, plus all of the standard abbreviations you're likely to encounter when working on any knitting project.

Basic Knitting Information

Standard Knitting Abbreviations

*	repeat whatever follows the * as indicated
[ ]	work directions in brackets the number of times specified.
A, B, C	color A, B, C
approx	approximately
beg	beginning
BO	bind off
CC	Contrast color
cn	cable needle
CO	cast on
cont	continue, continuing
dec	decrease
dpn(s)	double-pointed needle(s)
ea	each
est	establish, established
foll	following
inc	increase
k	knit
kfb	knit in front and back
k2tog	knit 2 together
kwise	knitwise, as if to knit
M1	make one stitch
MC	main color
mult	multiple
p	purl
pfb	purl in front and back
pm	place marker

(in) patt	(in pattern)
p2tog	purl 2 together
prev	previous
psso	pass slipped stitch over
pwise	purlwise
rem	remaining
rep	repeat
rnd	round
RS	right side
rep	repeat
SKP	slip 1, knit 1, pass slipped stitch over
sl	slip
SSK	slip slip knit
st(s)	stitch(es)
St st	Stockinette Stitch
tbl	through back loop
tog	together
WS	wrong side
w&t	wrap and turn
yo	yarn over

SPECIAL ABBREVIATIONS:

M1 (make one stitch) = Lift running thread before next stitch onto left needle and knit into the back loop.

SSK = Slip next 2 sts, one at a time, to right needle; insert point of left needle into the fronts of these 2 sts and knit them together from this position – dec made.

M1R: Make 1 right. Coming from the back, pick up strand between stitches and knit through the front.

M1L: Make 1 left. Coming from the front, pick up strand between stitches and knit through the back.

Standard Crochet Abbreviations

ch	chain
dc	double crochet
dtr	double triple crochet
hdc	half double crochet
hk	hook
lp(s)	loop, loops
sc	single crochet
tr	triple crochet

Knitting Needle Conversions

diameter (mm)	US size
2	0
2.25	1
2.5	1½
2.75	2
3	2½
3.25	3
3.5	4
3.75	5
4	6
4.5	7
5	8
5.5	9
6	10
6.5	10½
8	11
9	13
10	15
12.75	17
15	19
20	36

Hooks for Yarn Crochet

DIAMETER (MM)	US SIZE
2.25	B/1
2.75	C/2
3.25	D/3
3.5	E/4
3.75	F/5
4	G/6
5	H/8
5.5	I/9
6	J/10
6.5	K/10½
8	L/11
9	M/13, N/13
10	N/15, P/15
15	P/Q
16	Q
19	S

Hooks for Thread Crochet

DIAMETER (MM)	US SIZE
.75	14
.85	13
1	12
1.1	11
1.3	10
1.4	9
1.5	8
1.65	7
1.8	6
1.9	5
2	4
2.1	3
2.25	2
2.75	1
3.25	0
3.5	00

Yarn Weight Guidelines

Since the names given to different weights of yarn can vary widely depending on the country of origin or the yarn manufacturer's preference, the Craft Yarn Council of America has put together a standard yarn weight system to impose a bit of order on the sometimes unruly yarn labels. Look for a picture of a skein of yarn with a number 0–6 on most kinds of yarn to figure out its "official" weight. Gauge is given over 4" (10cm) of Stockinette stitch. The information in the chart below is taken from www.yarnstandards.com.

	Super Bulky(6)	Bulky (5)	Medium (4)	Light (3)	Fine (2)	Superfine (1)	Lace (0)
TYPE	bulky, roving	chunky, craft, rug	worsted, afghan, aran	dk, light, worsted	sport, baby	sock, fingering, baby	fingering, 10-count crochet thread
KNIT GAUGE RANGE	6–11 sts	12–15 sts	16–20 sts	21–24 sts	23–26 sts	27–32 sts	33–40 sts
RECOM-MENDED NEEDLE IN US SIZE RANGE	11 and larger	9 to 11	7 to 9	5 to 7	3 to 5	1 to 3	000 to 1

Substituting Yarn

If you substitute yarn, be sure to select a yarn of the same weight as the yarn recommended for the project. Even after checking that the recommended gauge on the yarn you plan to substitute is the same as for the yarn listed in the pattern, make sure to knit a swatch to ensure that the yarn and needles you are using will produce the correct gauge.

Basic Techniques

Long-Tail Cast-On

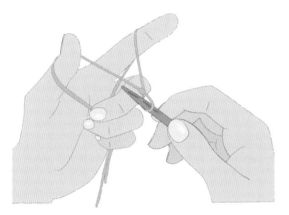

1 *Make a slip knot in your yarn, leaving enough of a tail for the number of stitches you need to cast on (about 1" (3cm) per stitch). Place the knot on one of your needles. Bring both ends of your yarn up between your thumb and index finger. Wrap one end around your thumb and the other around your finger, bringing both ends back down so you can control the tension with your other fingers.*

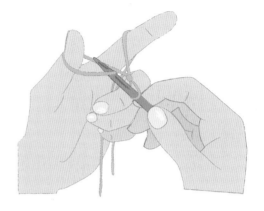

2 *Weave the needle tip up through the loop around your thumb.*

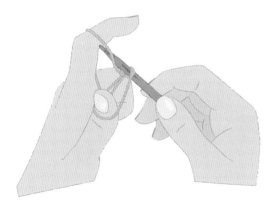

3 *Snag the string going up around your index finger with the tip of the needle.*

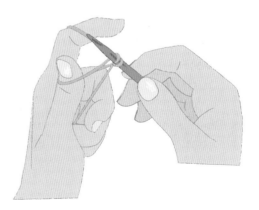

4 *Pull it back through the loop on your thumb and drop the loop off your thumb.*

Joining to Work in the Round (DPNs)

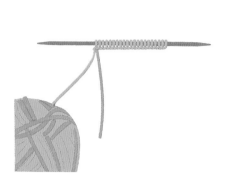 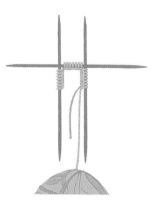 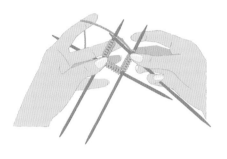

1 Cast all of the required stitches onto one dpn.

2 Divide the stitches evenly among all but one of the dpns.

3 Being careful not to twist the stitches, use the final dpn and the working yarn coming from the final cast-on stitch on the last needle, knit into the first stitch that you cast on.

Joining to Work in the Round (1 Circular Needle)

 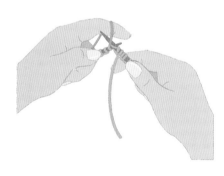

1 Cast on the required number of stitches.

2 Knit into the first stitch that you cast on.

Knitting Continental

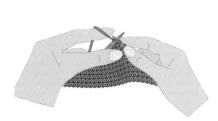  

1 With the working yarn in your left hand and above the first stitch on the front of your left needle, insert your right needle into the next stitch on your left needle from bottom to top/front to back.

2 Grab the working yarn with the tip of your right needle.

3 Pull it down through the stitch on the left needle, at the same time pulling that stitch off the left needle. You will be left with a new stitch on your right needle and one less stitch on your left.

Purling Continental

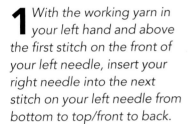   

1 Hold the yarn as for knitting, but insert the tip of your right needle through the next stitch on the left needle from top to bottom/back to front.

2 Grab the working yarn with the tip of your right needle.

3 Pull it back up through the stitch, at the same time pulling that stitch off the left needle. You're left with a new stitch on the right needle and one fewer on the left.

Make 1 Left (M1L)

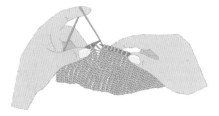 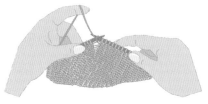 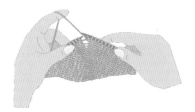

1 *Knit up to the point at which you'd like to make the increase. Insert your left needle from front to back underneath the bar between the stitch you just knit and the next one.*

2 *Insert the tip of your right needle into the back of the bar as if knitting into the back of a stitch and grab the working yarn.*

3 *Pull the yarn through the loop and onto the right needle, off the left needle.*

Make 1 Right (M1R)

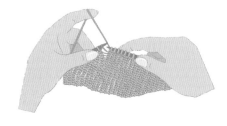 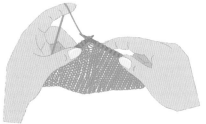 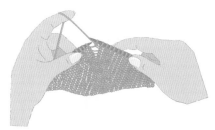

1 *Knit up to the point at which you'd like to make the increase. Insert your left needle from back to front underneath the bar between the stitch you just knit and the next one.*

2 *Insert the tip of your right needle into the front of the bar as if knitting a stitch and grab the working yarn.*

3 *Pull the yarn through the loop and onto the right needle, off the left needle.*

Knit 1 Front and Back (KFB)

  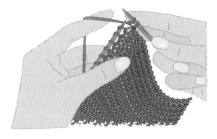

1 *Knit into the next stitch as usual, but don't pull it off the left needle.*

2 *Insert the right needle into the back of the same stitch from top to bottom.*

3 *Pull working yarn back through stitch and pull the stitch off the left needle.*

Slip Slip Knit (SSK)

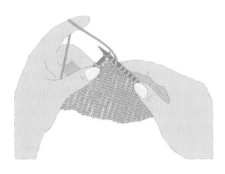 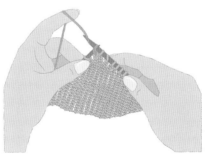 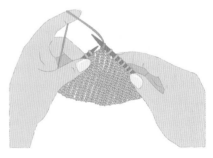

1 *Insert your right-hand needle into the next stitch as if to knit, but simply slip it off the left needle onto the right. Repeat for a second stitch.*

2 *Insert the tip of the left needle back through the two slipped stitches from left to right without pulling them off the right needle. Grab the working yarn with the tip of your right needle.*

3 *Pull the yarn through both stitches and off the left needle, leaving you with one stitch on your right needle instead of two.*

Knit 2 Together (K2tog)

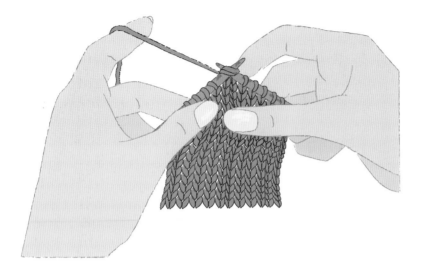

1 Treat the next two stitches on your left needle as one stitch, inserting the tip of your right needle into both stitches at the same time from bottom to top/front to back. Knit as usual and pull both stitches off the left needle.

Binding Off

1 Knit two stitches as usual.

2 Use the tip of your left needle to pull the first of the two stitches up over the second stitch and off the needle. One stitch bound off.

3 Knit another stitch and pull the second stitch up over the newest one and off the needle. Repeat to bind off as many stitches as required.

The top edge of this knit piece has been bound off.

Adding a Crochet Edge

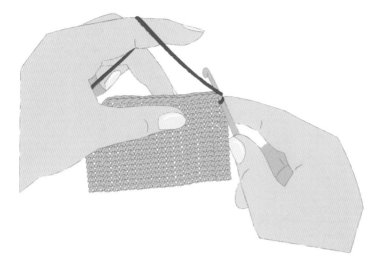

1 *Tie a slipknot around your crochet hook. Insert the tip of the crochet hook through the loops of one edge stitch.*

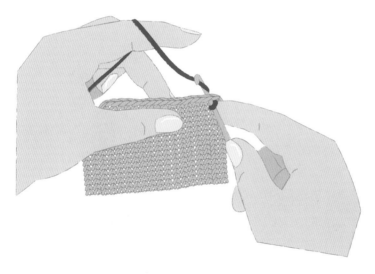

2 *Wrap the yarn around the tip of the crochet hook.*

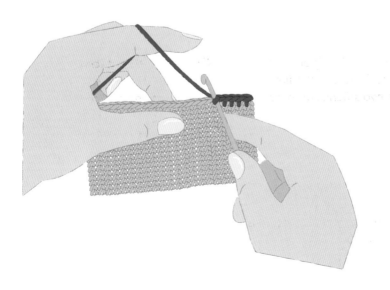

3 *Pull the yarn through both the edge stitch and the loop of the slipknot on the hook. You should have one loop left on the hook. Continue in this manner all along the edge to be crocheted.*

Conclusion

Producing *Knit and Crochet Now!* has been a fun and exhilarating adventure, and I hope you will enjoy the patterns in this book. Once you've whipped up a couple of pillows and an afghan, settle down on your couch with them as well as your knitting needles and yarn and join us for more episodes of the show. You can find us on your local public television station. We will continue to bring you a great program with fun and interesting projects and hope that you will spread the word to all your friends so they to can join us. For more information about *Knit and Crochet Now!* go to our web site, www.knitandcrochetnow.com.

Meet the Experts

Knit and Crochet Now! is blessed to have a wonderful host and exceptional experts every week on the show. As you can see from their biographies below they are indeed experts in their field.

Brett Bara

When Brett's not in front of the camera on *Knit and Crochet Now!* she is the Editor in Chief of *Crochet Today!* magazine. Before this, she was Crafts Editor at Woman's Day Special Interest Publications and a writer for numerous national magazines including *Marie Claire*, *Cosmopolitan*, *Details*, *Men's Health* and *Prevention*.

Brett has more than twenty years' experience as a crafter, and has been knitting and crocheting for over ten years. Her mission is to spread the joy of crafting far and wide, especially among the new generation of young DIYers. Brett also enjoys sewing, embroidery and anything crafty, in addition to DIY decorating, baking and vintage shopping. She lives in New York City, where she is writing a sewing book to be released in spring 2011.

Read Brett's blogs at www. CrochetToday.com and http://manhattancraftroom.blogspot.com or visit her Web site (www.brettbara. com). Follow her on Twitter under the name brettbara.

Robyn Chachula

Robyn Chachula's winding path to her crochet career began as most have not in the industry, but as a crafter. "So my day job, as an engineer, may seem like a far cry from crochet fashion design, but for me, they are one in the same. They both use my ability to take a big project and break it down into little items that I can understand, then piece them back together for the overall big picture." Her first published pattern was a simple leash created for Faye, her German shepherd. This spurred her on to start her own crochet design company, Crochet by Faye. She has been published in a number of national magazines and books, including *Interweave Crochet* and *Crochet Today!*

Her first crochet book is *Blueprint Crochet: Modern Designs for the Visual Crocheter*. Her pattern book, *Mission Falls Goes Crochet*, is available now from Mission Falls Yarn. You can see all of her architecturally inspired pieces at www. crochetbyfaye.com.

Drew Emborsky

Drew Emborsky's quirky title as "The Crochet Dude" and his kitschy tongue-in-cheek designs have propelled him from a young, unknown fiber artist to the cutting edge of the fiber design world. His unique role as a male knitter and crocheter has opened doors for other men who were stuck in the closet with their yarn, knitting needles, and crochet hooks.

Drew studied fine art at Kendall College of Art and Design in Grand Rapids, Michigan, and is a Professional member of the Crochet Guild of America where he has received a master certificate in crochet. He has been featured in national publications including *BUST Magazine* and *Crochet Today!*, as well as international newspapers like *The Sunday Telegraph* (in London). He co-authored *Men Who Knit and the Dogs Who Love Them* and his latest book of crocheted men's clothing designs is titled *The Crochet Dude's Designs for Guys*. Emborsky launched his Web site (www.drewemborsky.com) and blog in February, 2005, and has gained a loyal following throughout the world. Visit it at www.blog.thecrochetdude. com where Drew offers patterns and a peek at his day-to-day life. He lives in Houston, Texas with his two cats, Chandler and Cleopatra.

Kristin Nicholas

Kristin Nicholas learned to knit and sew when she was nine years old. She followed her passion for creating and received a B.S. from University of Delaware and M.S. from Colorado State University in Textiles and Clothing. She has worked in the American needlework industry for over twenty-five years as a Creative Director and Stitchery and Knitwear Designer. She is the author of eight books including *Color by Kristin*, *Knitting for Baby* and more. Her specialty is working with color and she is known as a color expert within the needlework industry. She has her own line of yarn, Julia, named for her daughter, and it is distributed throughout North America by Nashua Handknits.

Kristin lives on a working sheep farm in western Massachusetts with her husband and daughter. Her home and work has been featured in *Country Home*, *Country Living*, and many more national publications. She has been a knitting expert on *Knit and Crochet Now!* for the past three seasons.

You can learn more about Kristin by visiting her Web site (www.kristinnicholas.com/) and learn about life on a working sheep farm by following her blog (http://getting-stitched-on-the-farm.blogspot.com/).

Maggie Pace

Maggie Pace is owner and founder of the felted knit design company, Pick Up Sticks, which she started in 2003, when she was five months pregnant with her second child. After working as a journalist for ten years, Maggie was ready for something new. In keeping with family tradition—every female member of her family had a craft business going back two generations—and because she had just discovered felting, it seemed a logical career step.

Today Pick Up Sticks (www.pickupsticksonline.com) patterns and kits are sold at stores nationwide and Maggie has written two books on knitted felt, *Felt Forward* and *Felt It!* . Maggie was noted as a 2008 Women Entrepreneur for *Country Living* magazine. She has appeared on several national and local television programs, including DIY Network's *Knitty Gritty* and PBS's *Needle Arts Studio* with Shay Pendray. Maggie continues to design all the patterns and her mother Joan tests each one. The mother/daughter team runs the business from a little studio in Oakland, California.

Myra Wood

Myra Wood is an internationally known fiber & bead artist and designer. She teaches a wide range of classes in beading, embroidery, crochet and knitting, specializing in all things freeform. She's also appeared on several episodes of *Knitty Gritty* and *Uncommon Threads* for the DIY and HGTV networks along with publishing numerous crochet, knit, jewelry and wearable art patterns in a wide range of books and magazines. She's written two books: *Creative Crochet Lace* and *Crazy Lace, an Artistic Approach to Creative Lace Knitting*. Myra has been crocheting, sewing and crafting since she was young and enjoys any opportunity to inspire others creatively. She is also the moderator for the International Freeform Guild with over 2000 members worldwide and coordinator for their annual national shows. Galleries of her work can be seen at www.myrawood.com.

Resources

Boye Needle
1-888-588-2700
info@simplicity.com
www.simplicity.com/t-boye.aspx

Red Heart Yarns
Coats & Clark
Consumer Services
P.O. Box 12229
Greenville, SC 29612-0229
(800) 648-1479
www.redheart.com

Crochet by Faye
www.crochetbyfaye.com
info@crochetbyfaye.com

The Crochet Dude
www.drewemborsky.com

Getting Stitched on the Farm
http://getting-stitched-on-the-farm.blogspot.com/

Jimmy Beans Wool
5000 Smithridge Drive #A11
Reno NV 89502
(877) 529-5648
www.jimmybeanswool.com/
info@JimmyBeansWool.com

Knit and Crochet Now!
708 Gravenstein Hwy. #231
Sebastopol, CA 95472
www.knitandcrochetnow.com/
info@knitandcrochetnow.com

KristinNicholas.com
PO Box 212
Bernardston, MA 01337-0212
www.kristinnicholas.com/

Manhattan Craft Room
http://manhattancraftroom.blogspot.com

Myra Wood
www.myrawood.com
myra@myrawood.com

Pick Up Sticks
6267 Merced Avenue
Oakland, CA 94611
510-339-6807
www.pickupsticksonline.com
customerservice@pickupsticksonline.com

Index

Index

Index

Looking for more projects to knit now? Try one of these great knitting books.

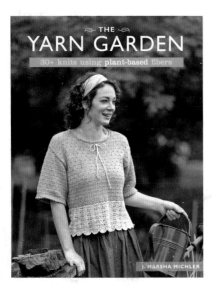

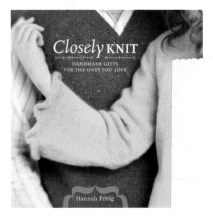

The Yarn Garden
30 Knits Using Plant-Based Fibers
J. Marsha Michler

The 30 beautiful patterns of *The Yarn Garden* show you the joys of working with plant-based yarns! From traditional favorites like cotton and linen to more exotic nettle and hemp, plant-based yarns are a joy to knit and offer unique benefits. Plant-based yarns are perfect for warm-weather knitting and boast a wide range of weights and textures. If you want to make eco-friendly and animal-product free projects, you'll find what you're looking for here.

ISBN-10: 0-89689-827-X
ISBN-13: 978-0-89689-827-1
SRN: Z2990

Knitted Homestyle
The Editors of The Art of Knitting Magazine

The editors of *The Art of Knitting Magazine* present you with a wealth of ideas for contemporary and stylish knit projects for your home. Packed inside you'll find a diverse range of home accessory projects, from knitted pictures, pillows and throws to pet blankets and egg cozies. Whether you're a novice knitter or are working on your hundredth project, *Knitted Homestyle* provides you with the clear technique instruction you'll need to make your home handknit-cozy.

ISBN-10: 0-7153-3313-5
ISBN-13: 978-0-7153-3313-6
SRN: Z5010

Closely Knit
Handmade Gifts
For The Ones You Love
Hannah Fettig

Closely Knit is filled with thoughtf[ul] knitted gifts to fit all the people yo[u] love: special handknits for mother[s,] daughters, sisters, the men in your life, precious wee ones and treasu[red] friends. From luxurious scarves an[d] wearable sweaters to cozy socks a[nd] even a quick-to-knit heart pin, the[re] really is something for everyone o[n] your list in this book. Projects ran[ge] from quick and simple to true labo[r] of love, and each is rated with a h[andy] time guide so you can choose wha[t to] knit based on how much time you[…] Bonus quick-fix options will save t[…] when you need to whip up a mea[ningful] gift in a jiffy.

ISBN-10: 1-60061-018-9
ISBN-13: 978-1-60061-018-9
SRN: Z1280